JUMBLE®
Health

These Puzzles Will Work Out Your Wits!

T0155164

**Henri Arnold,
Bob Lee,
David L. Hoyt,
and Jeff Knurek**

TRIUMPH
BOOKS

For further information, contact:
Triumph Books LLC
814 North Franklin Street
Chicago, Illinois 60610
Phone: (312) 337-0747
www.triumphbooks.com

Printed in U.S.A.

ISBN: 978-1-63727-085-1

Design by Sue Knopf

Contents

JUMBLE®
Health

Classic
Puzzles

JUMBLE®

Unscramble these four Jumbles, one letter
to each square, to form four ordinary words.

HARNC

LAUFT

SHEARE

MILDIP

WHAT THAT
PRECOCIOUSLY
BRIGHT BABY WAS.

NUCLEAR PHYSICS

Now arrange the circled letters
to form the surprise answer, as
suggested by the above cartoon.

**Print answer
here** A ◯◯◯◯◯ IN THE " ◯◯◯◯ "

JUMBLE®

Unscramble these four Jumbles, one letter to each square, to form four ordinary words.

APITO

FARIE

DIOING

TRAFOC

Thinks he's Izaac Walton

WHAT THE FISHING ENTHUSIAST WAS.

Now arrange the circled letters to form the surprise answer, as suggested by the above cartoon.

Print answer here A " ⬡⬡⬡⬡ – ⬡⬡⬡⬡⬡ "

JUMBLE®

Unscramble these four Jumbles, one letter to each square, to form four ordinary words.

WATHE

TRIDY

EMTYSS

SILFOS

I'm not sure he's ready yet

SHOULD A CAR WITH AUTOMATIC DRIVE BE ENTRUSTED TO SOME-ONE WHO'S THIS?

Now arrange the circled letters to form the surprise answer, as suggested by the above cartoon.

Print answer here " ◯◯◯◯◯◯◯◯◯◯ "

JUMBLE®

Unscramble these four Jumbles, one letter to each square, to form four ordinary words.

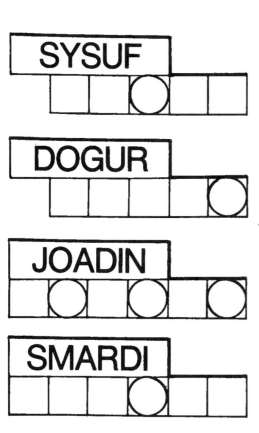

SYSUF

DOGUR

JOADIN

SMARDI

You might want to clean your room first

Are you kidding?!

WHAT A SPOILED BRAT DOES.

Now arrange the circled letters to form the surprise answer, as suggested by the above cartoon.

Print answer here " ☐☐ ' ☐ " HIS OWN ☐☐☐

JUMBLE®

Unscramble these four Jumbles, one letter
to each square, to form four ordinary words.

HESAF

LUTOC

EMBLUF

YARTTE

I'm just fine, but I don't
want any more of that beast

HORSEBACK RIDING
IS A SPORT THAT
SOMETIMES MAKES THE
NOVICE FEEL THIS.

Now arrange the circled letters
to form the surprise answer, as
suggested by the above cartoon.

Print answer here

JUMBLE®

Unscramble these four Jumbles, one letter to each square, to form four ordinary words.

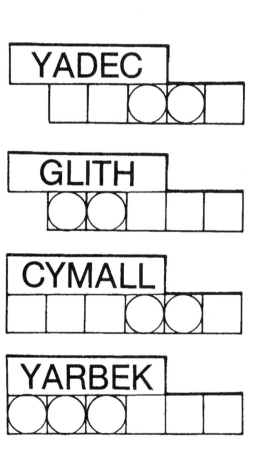

YADEC

GLITH

CYMALL

YARBEK

Someone is going to have to pay for this

WHAT THERE WAS PLENTY OF AFTER THE POST OFFICE CAUGHT FIRE.

Now arrange the circled letters to form the surprise answer, as suggested by the above cartoon.

Print answer here " ☐☐☐☐☐ ☐☐☐☐ "

JUMBLE®

Unscramble these four Jumbles, one letter to each square, to form four ordinary words.

EUQER

NAFTI

GIBNEN

TARNEK

Come along now

INVESTMENTS

HE THINKS HE'S GOING PLACES WHEN HE'S REALLY THIS.

Now arrange the circled letters to form the surprise answer, as suggested by the above cartoon.

Print answer here ☐☐☐☐☐ " ☐☐☐☐☐ "

JUMBLE®

Unscramble these four Jumbles, one letter to each square, to form four ordinary words.

DARUG

THICH

SCYTIK

CYSTOL

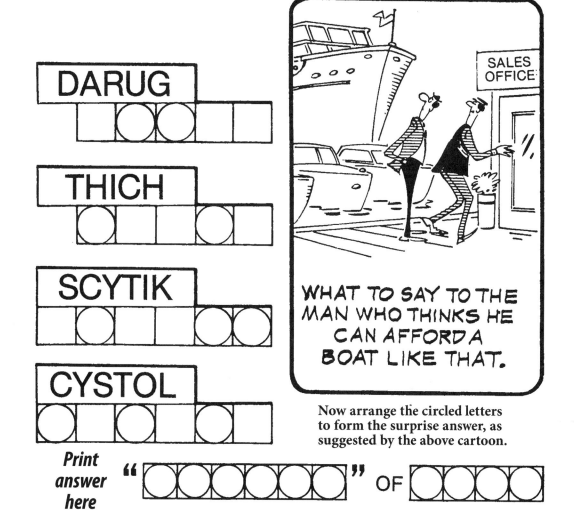

SALES OFFICE

WHAT TO SAY TO THE MAN WHO THINKS HE CAN AFFORD A BOAT LIKE THAT.

Now arrange the circled letters to form the surprise answer, as suggested by the above cartoon.

Print answer here " ◯◯◯◯◯◯ " OF ◯◯◯◯

JUMBLE®

Unscramble these four Jumbles, one letter to each square, to form four ordinary words.

CRAID

UFYSS

LARTEY

PREEMT

NASA PERSONNEL OFFICE

HE WANTED TO BE AN ASTRONAUT, BUT THEY SAID ALL HE HAD TAKEN UP IN SCHOOL WAS THIS.

Now arrange the circled letters to form the surprise answer, as suggested by the above cartoon.

Print answer here " ◯◯◯◯◯ "

JUMBLE®

Unscramble these four Jumbles, one letter
to each square, to form four ordinary words.

NOPIA

PUTIL

TUILGY

UPDINT

Aren't you supposed to
be watching what
you eat?

A DIET IS SOME-
THING YOU KEEP
PUTTING OFF WHILE
YOU KEEP THIS.

Now arrange the circled letters
to form the surprise answer, as
suggested by the above cartoon.

Print answer here

11

JUMBLE®

Unscramble these four Jumbles, one letter to each square, to form four ordinary words.

PAROE

NOMUT

GENPOS

REPHEL

WHAT THAT TALL
BEACHCOMBER WAS.

Now arrange the circled letters to form the surprise answer, as suggested by the above cartoon.

Print answer here A ☐☐☐☐☐ " ☐☐☐☐☐☐☐☐☐☐ "

JUMBLE®

Unscramble these four Jumbles, one letter
to each square, to form four ordinary words.

INGIC

LUGIE

SNIULF

MARLOF

I worked my head off
today, but I made us
a lot of money

PEOPLE WHO GO ALL
OUT OFTEN END
UP THIS WAY.

Now arrange the circled letters
to form the surprise answer, as
suggested by the above cartoon.

Print answer here

JUMBLE®

Unscramble these four Jumbles, one letter
to each square, to form four ordinary words.

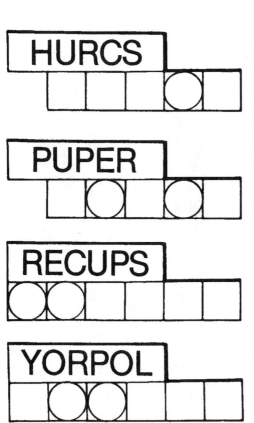

HURCS

PUPER

RECUPS

YORPOL

I'm down here, Harold

AN ELOPEMENT SOMETIMES RESULTS WHEN MAN PROPOSES AND FUTURE MOTHER-IN-LAW DOES THIS.

Now arrange the circled letters
to form the surprise answer, as
suggested by the above cartoon.

Print answer here

JUMBLE®

Unscramble these four Jumbles, one letter to each square, to form four ordinary words.

TROIB

PYLAP

CHERAG

YAMBIG

CANDLES ON BIRTHDAY CAKES HELP PEOPLE MAKE THIS.

Now arrange the circled letters to form the surprise answer, as suggested by the above cartoon.

Print answer here " ◯◯◯◯◯ " OF THEIR ◯◯◯

JUMBLE®

Unscramble these four Jumbles, one letter
to each square, to form four ordinary words.

EUNEQ

KYDUS

TARBUL

GUMSED

HOW AUTOMOBILES
MOVED BEFORE ANY-
ONE THOUGHT OF USING
LUBRICATING OIL.

Now arrange the circled letters
to form the surprise answer, as
suggested by the above cartoon.

Print answer here THEY JUST ⬭⬭⬭⬭⬭⬭⬭⬭ BY

JUMBLE®

Unscramble these four Jumbles, one letter
to each square, to form four ordinary words.

KNALF
◻◯◯◻◻

EVVAL
◻◻◻◯◯

THARRE
◻◻◻◯◻◯◯

YABSUW
◯◻◯◻◻◯

WHAT'S THE ENVI-
RONMENT LIKE WHEN
YOU SLEEP ALONG-
SIDE YOUR HORSE?

Now arrange the circled letters
to form the surprise answer, as
suggested by the above cartoon.

Print answer here ◯◯◯◯ ◯◯◯◯◯◯

JUMBLE®

Unscramble these four Jumbles, one letter
to each square, to form four ordinary words.

ENCAP

DRUGO

RUNUTE

WHEPEN

I'm not surprised

CLOSED

WHAT HAPPENED TO
THE RESTAURANT
THAT SERVED THOSE
SUBSTANDARD SUB-
MARINE SANDWICHES?

Now arrange the circled letters
to form the surprise answer, as
suggested by the above cartoon.

Print answer here IT ◯◯◯◯◯ ◯◯◯◯◯◯

JUMBLE®

Unscramble these four Jumbles, one letter
to each square, to form four ordinary words.

MERIG

PRUNS

NELKEN

TINISS

WHAT THE COPS
LOOKED FOR WHEN
THERE WAS A
ROBBERY AT THE
SAUSAGE FACTORY.

Now arrange the circled letters
to form the surprise answer, as
suggested by the above cartoon.

Print
answer
here

THE 〇〇〇〇〇〇〇 " 〇〇〇〇 "

JUMBLE®

Unscramble these four Jumbles, one letter to each square, to form four ordinary words.

DAGLE

TARAP

OKOCIE

HOGUNE

WHAT THOSE STRAY DOGS ENJOYED MOST AT DINNERTIME.

Now arrange the circled letters to form the surprise answer, as suggested by the above cartoon.

Print answer here " ⬡⬡⬡⬡⬡⬡ " ⬡⬡⬡⬡

JUMBLE®

Unscramble these four Jumbles, one letter
to each square, to form four ordinary words.

BECAL

PUROG

AMBALS

SNUFUG

WHAT THAT
HEROIC FIREMAN
BECAME.

Now arrange the circled letters
to form the surprise answer, as
suggested by the above cartoon.

Print answer here " ◯◯◯◯◯◯◯ "

JUMBLE®

Unscramble these four Jumbles, one letter
to each square, to form four ordinary words.

LEEXI

APLLE

INPROS

PLOMYC

USED
TIRES

SALE

WHAT YOU MIGHT
FIND AT THAT
MOM AND POP
TIRE SHOP.

Now arrange the circled letters
to form the surprise answer, as
suggested by the above cartoon.

Print answer here A " "

JUMBLE®

Unscramble these four Jumbles, one letter to each square, to form four ordinary words.

NONAY

DAPIL

LAPLOW

INTEWG

Dear, why don't you get someone to help you?

WHAT YOU MIGHT END UP WITH FROM TOO MUCH HOUSE-CLEANING.

Now arrange the circled letters to form the surprise answer, as suggested by the above cartoon.

Print answer here   A ◯◯◯◯◯◯ "◯◯◯◯"

JUMBLE®

Unscramble these four Jumbles, one letter
to each square, to form four ordinary words.

RILLT

UGGOE

UMCAUV

CELEEF

I can't tell one finny creature from the other

WHAT YOU MIGHT DO WITH THE MENU WHEN YOU'RE DINING AT A FISH RESTAURANT.

Now arrange the circled letters
to form the surprise answer, as
suggested by the above cartoon.

Print answer
here   " ◯◯◯◯◯◯ " ◯◯◯◯

JUMBLE®

Unscramble these four Jumbles, one letter
to each square, to form four ordinary words.

NARBD

ZEFOR

LIZZES

FICTEN

Who
is
he?

!

HE WENT
UNRECOGNIZED WHEN
HE HAD THIS.

Now arrange the circled letters
to form the surprise answer, as
suggested by the above cartoon.

Print answer here HIS " ◯◯◯ " ◯◯◯◯◯◯◯

JUMBLE®

Unscramble these four Jumbles, one letter
to each square, to form four ordinary words.

UGGEA

EBILE

SERBIC

NITDAY

WHEN THE PRICE OF
SUGAR ESCALATED,
THE CUSTOMERS
DID THIS.

Now arrange the circled letters
to form the surprise answer, as
suggested by the above cartoon.

**Print answer
here** ☐☐☐☐☐☐ " ☐☐☐☐ "

JUMBLE®
Health

Daily
Puzzles

JUMBLE®

Unscramble these four Jumbles, one letter
to each square, to form four ordinary words.

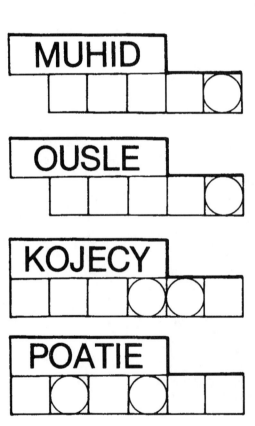

MUHID

OUSLE

KOJECY

POATIE

You don't look so good

HOW HE FELT WHEN
HE FINALLY REACHED
THE VERY TOP OF
THE MOUNTAIN.

Now arrange the circled letters
to form the surprise answer, as
suggested by the above cartoon.

Print answer here

JUMBLE®

Unscramble these four Jumbles, one letter to each square, to form four ordinary words.

SESCH

EFTUL

KIALLA

ROYSAR

WHAT THE CHAMPION MALTED MILK MAKER THOUGHT HE GOT WHEN THE BOSS GAVE HIM A BONUS.

Now arrange the circled letters to form the surprise answer, as suggested by the above cartoon.

Print answer here A 〇〇〇〇 " 〇〇〇〇〇 "

JUMBLE®

Unscramble these four Jumbles, one letter
to each square, to form four ordinary words.

RUPEN

ELROD

YIVERF

TORMAR

EVERY TIME HE RAN
TWO HUNDRED YARDS,
HE ACTUALLY ONLY
DID THIS.

Now arrange the circled letters
to form the surprise answer, as
suggested by the above cartoon.

Print answer here ⬡⬡⬡⬡⬡ TWO ⬡⬡⬡⬡

JUMBLE®

Unscramble these four Jumbles, one letter
to each square, to form four ordinary words.

LECEX
◯◯□◯◯

NIDEK
◯□□◯◯

CUROGH
◯◯□□□◯

WARTOD
◯□□□◯◯

AFTER GETTING TWO
COLLEGE DIPLOMAS, HE
LED A LIFE OF
CRIME UNTIL THE
COPS THREATENED
HIM WITH THIS.

Now arrange the circled letters
to form the surprise answer, as
suggested by the above cartoon.

Print
answer
here

A ◯◯◯◯◯◯ ◯◯◯◯◯◯

JUMBLE®

Unscramble these four Jumbles, one letter to each square, to form four ordinary words.

BODUT

PEDYT

ENGLIS

YURTIP

Son, you're going to succeed me some day. I want you to know all about it

THE ONLY WAY TO LEARN THE COFFEE BUSINESS.

Now arrange the circled letters to form the surprise answer, as suggested by the above cartoon.

Print answer here

FROM THE " ⃝⃝⃝⃝⃝⃝⃝ " ⃝⃝

JUMBLE®

Unscramble these four Jumbles, one letter to each square, to form four ordinary words.

IFFYT

OGGRE

RENUDE

CARCIT

Now we're all set for our new home where it's warm

USED TIRES

RETREADS ARE SOLD FOR PEOPLE WHO WANT TO DO THIS.

Now arrange the circled letters to form the surprise answer, as suggested by the above cartoon.

Print answer here "◯◯ – ◯◯◯◯"

JUMBLE®

Unscramble these four Jumbles, one letter to each square, to form four ordinary words.

VABOE

ARBIN

LEWOLF

FLUTAR

WHEN YOU BUY A HERD OF BISON, YOU CAN EXPECT TO RECEIVE THIS.

Now arrange the circled letters to form the surprise answer, as suggested by the above cartoon.

Print answer here A ⬡⬡⬡⬡⬡⬡⬡ " ⬡⬡⬡⬡ "

JUMBLE®

Unscramble these four Jumbles, one letter
to each square, to form four ordinary words.

PETIR
◻◻◻○○

WORNC
○◻◻◻◻

TRYSOF
◻◻○○◻◻

UNCHAP
◻◻◻◻◻○

WHAT THEY SERVED
IN THAT RESTAURANT
FAVORED BY THE
KARATE CROWD.

Now arrange the circled letters
to form the surprise answer, as
suggested by the above cartoon.

Print answer here " ○○○○○ "

JUMBLE®

Unscramble these four Jumbles, one letter
to each square, to form four ordinary words.

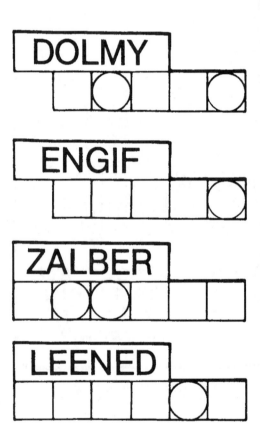

DOLMY

ENGIF

ZALBER

LEENED

You're no longer by
yourself—you have us!

BANK

THAT FRIENDLY
NEIGHBORHOOD BANK
CATERED TO PEOPLE
WHO WERE THIS.

Now arrange the circled letters
to form the surprise answer, as
suggested by the above cartoon.

Print answer here " ⬡⬡⬡⬡⬡ – ⬡⬡ "

JUMBLE®

Unscramble these four Jumbles, one letter
to each square, to form four ordinary words.

PANCO

WENIT

DRAWZI

QUESMO

WHY PILLOWS ARE
SO EXPENSIVE.

Now arrange the circled letters
to form the surprise answer, as
suggested by the above cartoon.

Print answer here

JUMBLE®

Unscramble these four Jumbles, one letter
to each square, to form four ordinary words.

OUMES

SATTY

REGLED

PERRIM

WHAT THEY WERE
AWARDED AT THE
GRADUATION CERE-
MONIES AT DIVING
SCHOOL.

Now arrange the circled letters
to form the surprise answer, as
suggested by the above cartoon.

Print answer here "◯◯◯◯◯ - ◯◯◯◯◯◯"

JUMBLE®

Unscramble these four Jumbles, one letter
to each square, to form four ordinary words.

YEJON

MIRPE

CLIPSE

ARXOTH

IS THIS THE BEST
LUBRICANT FOR
FURNITURE WHEELS?

Now arrange the circled letters
to form the surprise answer, as
suggested by the above cartoon.

Print answer here " ⃝⃝⃝⃝⃝⃝ " ⃝⃝⃝

JUMBLE®

Unscramble these four Jumbles, one letter
to each square, to form four ordinary words.

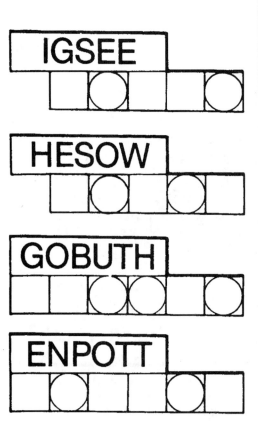

IGSEE

HESOW

GOBUTH

ENPOTT

HONEST AL'S

THE SMOOTHEST
RUNNING THING
ABOUT THAT CAR.

Now arrange the circled letters
to form the surprise answer, as
suggested by the above cartoon.

Print answer here

JUMBLE®

Unscramble these four Jumbles, one letter
to each square, to form four ordinary words.

WHOYS

MAORA

PELPIN

ALFELN

Thank you, Sir Walter

ANOTHER NAME
FOR CHIVALRY.

Now arrange the circled letters
to form the surprise answer, as
suggested by the above cartoon.

Print answer here " ◯◯◯◯ " ◯◯◯◯◯◯◯

JUMBLE®

Unscramble these four Jumbles, one letter
to each square, to form four ordinary words.

TRUIF

KONET

SACCUT

DRIZAL

You'd think they'd look it up
in the encyclopedia

WHAT'S MISSING
FROM MOST HOT
DISPUTES?

Now arrange the circled letters
to form the surprise answer, as
suggested by the above cartoon.

Print answer here

JUMBLE®

Unscramble these four Jumbles, one letter
to each square, to form four ordinary words.

SCERS

LYGUL

TALNED

NERBAN

We're having an explosively
good time

WHAT THE
DYNAMITERS'
ANNUAL SHINDIG
WAS.

Now arrange the circled letters
to form the surprise answer, as
suggested by the above cartoon.

Print answer here   A ⬡⬡⬡⬡⬡ ⬡⬡⬡⬡⬡

JUMBLE®

Unscramble these four Jumbles, one letter
to each square, to form four ordinary words.

KECHE

LOBEN

SEWBOT

NAIVED

Oops!

My dear, you'll
never believe what
Mildred did next...

ANOTHER THING
THAT PEOPLE ARE
ALWAYS SPILLING.

Now arrange the circled letters
to form the surprise answer, as
suggested by the above cartoon.

Print answer here

JUMBLE®

Unscramble these four Jumbles, one letter
to each square, to form four ordinary words.

KNACS

TOYBO

EPITOC

RANCOB

THAT HUSBAND
AND WIFE KNEW
EACH OTHER LIKE
A BOOK---

Now arrange the circled letters
to form the surprise answer, as
suggested by the above cartoon.

*Print answer
here*

JUMBLE®

Unscramble these four Jumbles, one letter to each square, to form four ordinary words.

KLUFE

ATAGE

RAHWTT

DUSHOL

Did I disturb you, Mary Ann?

Oh, no! I am just taking a bath and trying to wash my hair

SOMETHING ONE'S IN WHEN ONE'S NOT IN ANYTHING ELSE.

Now arrange the circled letters to form the surprise answer, as suggested by the above cartoon.

Print answer here THE ⭕⭕⭕⭕⭕⭕⭕⭕⭕⭕⭕⭕

JUMBLE®

Unscramble these four Jumbles, one letter
to each square, to form four ordinary words.

OCCIL

WARBL

AGMANE

BROSAB

WHAT BUILDING
THAT BIG TUNNEL
MUST HAVE BEEN.

Now arrange the circled letters
to form the surprise answer, as
suggested by the above cartoon.

Print answer here ☐ "☐☐☐ "☐☐☐☐ "

JUMBLE®

Unscramble these four Jumbles, one letter
to each square, to form four ordinary words.

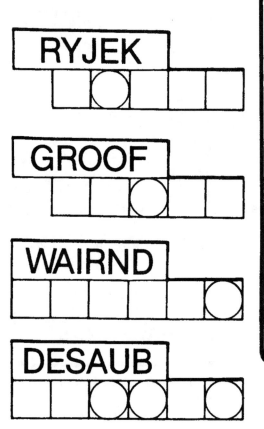

RYJEK

GROOF

WAIRND

DESAUB

THE SELFISH FARM-
HAND HAD TROUBLE
MILKING THE COW,
BECAUSE HE HAD NO
REGARD FOR THE
FEELING OF THIS.

Now arrange the circled letters
to form the surprise answer, as
suggested by the above cartoon.

Print answer here "  "

JUMBLE®

Unscramble these four Jumbles, one letter to each square, to form four ordinary words.

URSOE

TIPAL

PHONIS

SAWLAY

HOW TO MAIL
AN UMBRELLA.

Now arrange the circled letters to form the surprise answer, as suggested by the above cartoon.

Print answer here   BY "⬡⬡⬡⬡⬡⬡⬡⬡" ⬡⬡⬡⬡

JUMBLE®

Unscramble these four Jumbles, one letter to each square, to form four ordinary words.

BYRIN

GUZAE

LEPPUR

ENDECT

THE DIARY IS THE BOOK WHERE ALL HER SECRETS ARE THIS.

Now arrange the circled letters to form the surprise answer, as suggested by the above cartoon.

Print answer here " ⬡⬡⬡⬡⬡⬡ " ⬡⬡

JUMBLE®

Unscramble these four Jumbles, one letter
to each square, to form four ordinary words.

GLEEY

YOHBB

THOUPS

DUGIED

WHAT THE ANT DID
WHEN HE SAW THE
ANTEATER.

Now arrange the circled letters
to form the surprise answer, as
suggested by the above cartoon.

Print answer here

JUMBLE®

Unscramble these four Jumbles, one letter
to each square, to form four ordinary words.

DELAL

ORXYP

UNBRAU

CYTHAC

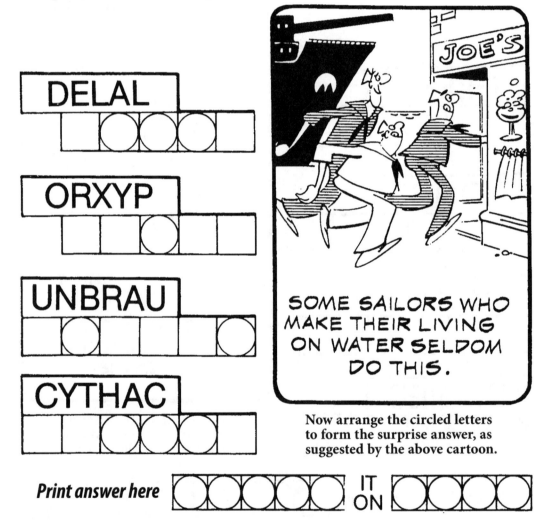

SOME SAILORS WHO
MAKE THEIR LIVING
ON WATER SELDOM
DO THIS.

Now arrange the circled letters
to form the surprise answer, as
suggested by the above cartoon.

Print answer here ⬡⬡⬡⬡⬡ IT
ON ⬡⬡⬡⬡⬡

JUMBLE®

Unscramble these four Jumbles, one letter
to each square, to form four ordinary words.

INNOO

TEBER

CLOUNK

NAHRGE

HER CHOICE OF
HUSBAND SHOWED
BETTER TASTE
THAN THIS.

Now arrange the circled letters
to form the surprise answer, as
suggested by the above cartoon.

Print answer here

JUMBLE®

Unscramble these four Jumbles, one letter
to each square, to form four ordinary words.

KEEVO

RAWLD

PANOWE

ERRTAY

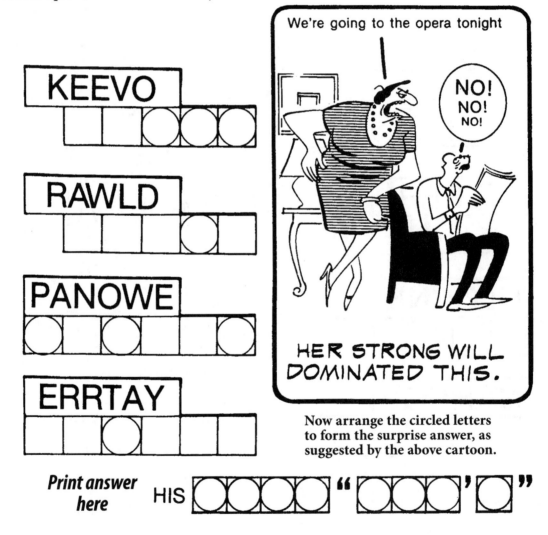

We're going to the opera tonight

NO!
NO!
NO!

HER STRONG WILL
DOMINATED THIS.

Now arrange the circled letters
to form the surprise answer, as
suggested by the above cartoon.

Print answer
here   HIS ⟨ ⟩⟨ ⟩⟨ ⟩⟨ ⟩⟨ ⟩ " ⟨ ⟩⟨ ⟩⟨ ⟩ ' ⟨ ⟩ "

JUMBLE®

Unscramble these four Jumbles, one letter to each square, to form four ordinary words.

NAISE

SIDAY

BEFILE

MOUFAS

Guess SHE'S going to do the proposing

WOMEN USE PERFUME BECAUSE SOME MEN ARE EASILY THIS.

Now arrange the circled letters to form the surprise answer, as suggested by the above cartoon.

Print answer here ⬡⬡⬡ BY THE ⬡⬡⬡⬡

JUMBLE®

Unscramble these four Jumbles, one letter
to each square, to form four ordinary words.

KANCK

ECHLE

NUCHEQ

DEGUBB

CURES
LUM-BAGO
ROOM-A-TISM
GOUT
SEE-ATICA
COLDS
SADDLE SORES
SORE THROAT

SALOON

PATENT MEDICINES
WERE SELDOM
WHAT THEY
WERE THIS.

Now arrange the circled letters
to form the surprise answer, as
suggested by the above cartoon.

Print answer " ⬚⬚⬚⬚⬚⬚⬚⬚ " UP
here   TO ⬚⬚

JUMBLE®

Unscramble these four Jumbles, one letter
to each square, to form four ordinary words.

PHACT

INYPP

ROZNEF

OANNEY

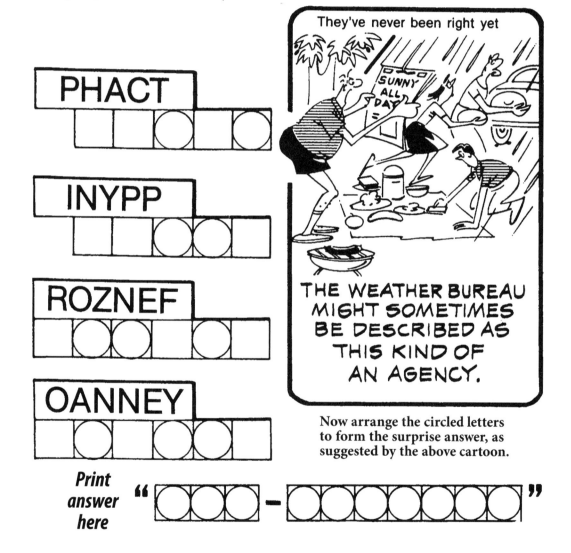

They've never been right yet

THE WEATHER BUREAU
MIGHT SOMETIMES
BE DESCRIBED AS
THIS KIND OF
AN AGENCY.

Now arrange the circled letters
to form the surprise answer, as
suggested by the above cartoon.

Print
answer
here

"☐☐☐ - ☐☐☐☐☐☐☐"

JUMBLE®

Unscramble these four Jumbles, one letter
to each square, to form four ordinary words.

NEFIT

INGGA

BALGER

ENGALT

He's going to get elected

And then he'll rob us blind

IN A POLITICIAN, THE GIFT OF GAB IS OFTEN CONNECT-ED WITH THIS.

Now arrange the circled letters
to form the surprise answer, as
suggested by the above cartoon.

Print answer here THE ⭕⭕⭕⭕⭕ OF ⭕⭕⭕⭕

JUMBLE®

Unscramble these four Jumbles, one letter
to each square, to form four ordinary words.

GOBUH

YACKT

EGWAIH

CHURCO

YOU were right, dear,
and I was wrong

WHAT A MAN
ACTUALLY EATS
WHEN HE SWALLOWS
HIS PRIDE.

Now arrange the circled letters
to form the surprise answer, as
suggested by the above cartoon.

Print answer here "  "

JUMBLE®

Unscramble these four Jumbles, one letter
to each square, to form four ordinary words.

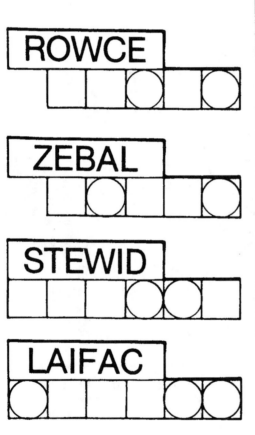

ROWCE

ZEBAL

STEWID

LAIFAC

STOCKS
BONDS

IN WALL STREET, SO-
CALLED "GOOD BUYS"
SOMETIMES TURN
OUT TO BE THIS.

Now arrange the circled letters
to form the surprise answer, as
suggested by the above cartoon.

Print answer here

JUMBLE®

Unscramble these four Jumbles, one letter to each square, to form four ordinary words.

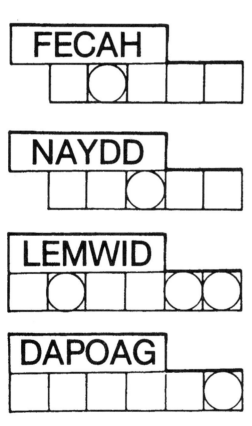

FECAH

NAYDD

LEMWID

DAPOAG

Compare that with the life you force ME to live!

But who needs his problems?

A COMPLAINT THAT USUALLY COMES FROM SOUR GRAPES.

Now arrange the circled letters to form the surprise answer, as suggested by the above cartoon.

Print answer here  " 〇〇〇〇〇 "

61

JUMBLE®

Unscramble these four Jumbles, one letter
to each square, to form four ordinary words.

ANUDT

CHOAV

SISALA

GLACEY

Hope they don't regret it

THERE WOULD BE
FEWER CASES OF
LOVE AT FIRST
SIGHT, IF THERE
WERE MORE PEOPLE
GIFTED WITH THIS.

Now arrange the circled letters
to form the surprise answer, as
suggested by the above cartoon.

**Print answer
here**

JUMBLE®

Unscramble these four Jumbles, one letter to each square, to form four ordinary words.

IRYAH

RIMON

DEGEWD

NIFTIE

They say her father owns half the town

WHAT THAT BATHING BEAUTY WAS WORTH.

Now arrange the circled letters to form the surprise answer, as suggested by the above cartoon.

Print answer here " ⬡⬡⬡⬡⬡⬡ " ⬡⬡⬡

JUMBLE

Unscramble these four Jumbles, one letter
to each square, to form four ordinary words.

NOPEY

UNORM

BONDEY

ZELPUZ

IF YOU WATCH
TOO MUCH FOOTBALL,
YOU MIGHT WEAR
OUT THIS.

Now arrange the circled letters
to form the surprise answer, as
suggested by the above cartoon.

*Print answer
here* YOUR " ◯◯◯ " ◯◯◯◯

JUMBLE®

Unscramble these four Jumbles, one letter
to each square, to form four ordinary words.

SAYES

OPYPP

AROTTE

PAPNYS

Best to let him think
it was his idea

A WOMAN MAY BE
THE REASON WHY
A MAN SUPPOSES
HE DOES THIS.

Now arrange the circled letters
to form the surprise answer, as
suggested by the above cartoon.

Print answer here

JUMBLE®

Unscramble these four Jumbles, one letter
to each square, to form four ordinary words.

ATQUO

RUHTT

RUGBBY

MENECT

WHAT THE ROULETTE
WHEEL TOOK FOR
A CHANGE.

Now arrange the circled letters
to form the surprise answer, as
suggested by the above cartoon.

Print
answer   A ⬡⬡⬡⬡ FOR " ⬡⬡⬡⬡⬡⬡ "
here   THE

JUMBLE®

Unscramble these four Jumbles, one letter to each square, to form four ordinary words.

JEGUD

EMICH

NEXETT

CAVIDE

WHAT HAPPENED WHEN FOUR COUPLES WENT TO A RESTAURANT?

Now arrange the circled letters to form the surprise answer, as suggested by the above cartoon.

Print answer here

JUMBLE®

Unscramble these four Jumbles, one letter to each square, to form four ordinary words.

LORBI

CUEJI

LOUGEY

BOOMAB

Shut up and keep chewing

WHAT LITTLE WHALES LIKE BEST.

Now arrange the circled letters to form the surprise answer, as suggested by the above cartoon.

Print answer " ⃝⃝⃝⃝⃝⃝⃝ " ⃝⃝⃝
here

JUMBLE®

Unscramble these four Jumbles, one letter
to each square, to form four ordinary words.

DORBO

TRIHM

WALTOU

RYCKIT

Arf!

WHAT THEY CALLED
THE HARDWARE
STORE'S CAT.

Now arrange the circled letters
to form the surprise answer, as
suggested by the above cartoon.

Print answer here   THE " ◯◯◯◯◯ ◯◯◯ "

JUMBLE®

Unscramble these four Jumbles, one letter to each square, to form four ordinary words.

OCTEM

HIWGE

ENOMAY

GAUHTT

Can't make the sauce without it

WHY THE COOK HURRIED TO THE HERB GARDEN.

Now arrange the circled letters to form the surprise answer, as suggested by the above cartoon.

Print answer here

HE HADN'T ⬡⬡⬡⬡ " ⬡⬡⬡⬡⬡ "

JUMBLE®

Unscramble these four Jumbles, one letter to each square, to form four ordinary words.

USEED

DAHYN

CAPELA

BOREEF

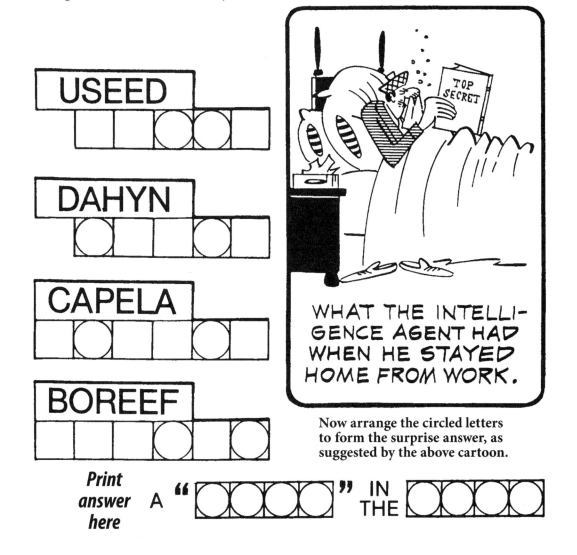

WHAT THE INTELLI-
GENCE AGENT HAD
WHEN HE STAYED
HOME FROM WORK.

Now arrange the circled letters to form the surprise answer, as suggested by the above cartoon.

Print answer here   A " ⬡⬡⬡⬡ " IN THE ⬡⬡⬡⬡

JUMBLE®

Unscramble these four Jumbles, one letter
to each square, to form four ordinary words.

LOBAT

TYMPE

SHAPIR

POMSIE

WHAT THE TREE
THAT EVERYONE
GATHERED UNDER
WAS CALLED.

Now arrange the circled letters
to form the surprise answer, as
suggested by the above cartoon.

Print answer here " ☐☐☐☐ ' ☐☐☐☐ "

JUMBLE®

Unscramble these four Jumbles, one letter
to each square, to form four ordinary words.

VEYHA

THOUY

SULTES

INDOWS

HIS APTITUDE FOR
PLATITUDE CREATES
THIS IN HIS
AUDIENCE.

Now arrange the circled letters
to form the surprise answer, as
suggested by the above cartoon.

Print answer here

JUMBLE®

Unscramble these four Jumbles, one letter
to each square, to form four ordinary words.

MORRA

CNOTH

LOWALT

DEEMLY

You're gorgeous!

Harold!

WOMEN DETEST FLAT-
TERY, ESPECIALLY
WHEN IT'S DIRECTED
TOWARDS THIS.

Now arrange the circled letters
to form the surprise answer, as
suggested by the above cartoon.

Print answer here

JUMBLE®

Unscramble these four Jumbles, one letter to each square, to form four ordinary words.

ALZEH
☐☐☐◯◯

BOMIL
☐☐☐◯◯

LAUTAC
☐☐☐◯☐☐

NERRED
☐☐◯◯☐◯

I don't see any bargains here

Looks like a rip-off to me

A FIRE SALE IS A PLACE WHERE BARGAIN HUNTERS MIGHT GET THIS.

Now arrange the circled letters to form the surprise answer, as suggested by the above cartoon.

Print answer here " ◯◯◯◯◯◯ "

JUMBLE®

Unscramble these four Jumbles, one letter
to each square, to form four ordinary words.

BUJOM

CITOX

SHORCC

PACRIY

Tee
hee

SOMETHING OFTEN
FOUND IN NEWS-
PAPERS AND ON
BEACHES.

Now arrange the circled letters
to form the surprise answer, as
suggested by the above cartoon.

*Print
answer
here* A ⬡⬡⬡⬡⬡ " ⬡⬡⬡⬡⬡ "

JUMBLE®

Unscramble these four Jumbles, one letter to each square, to form four ordinary words.

LAFAT

YIZZD

FROMIN

TIPIDE

If you had behaved yourself, this wouldn't have been necessary

A SURGEON MIGHT HAVE TO CUT OUT SOMETHING BECAUSE THE PATIENT THIS.

Now arrange the circled letters to form the surprise answer, as suggested by the above cartoon.

Print answer here

JUMBLE®

Unscramble these four Jumbles, one letter
to each square, to form four ordinary words.

ALYMN

GLIEB

FEXNAL

TESACK

MOST PEOPLE ARE
PUT OUT WHEN
THEY'RE THIS.

Now arrange the circled letters
to form the surprise answer, as
suggested by the above cartoon.

Print answer here " ⬡⬡⬡⬡⬡ ⬡⬡ "

JUMBLE®

Unscramble these four Jumbles, one letter to each square, to form four ordinary words.

MOVEN

SEMYS

DREHWS

LOUTTE

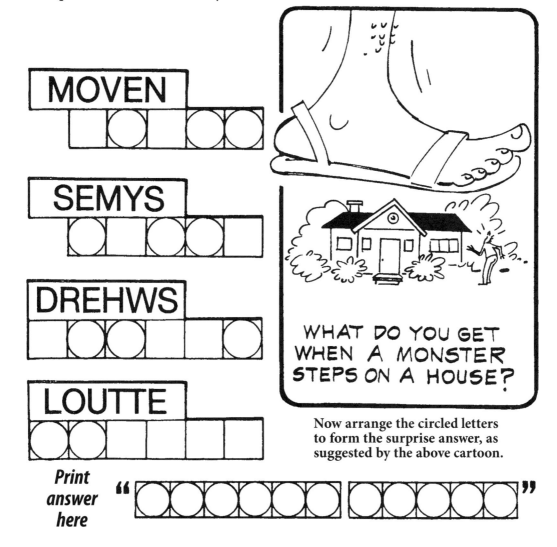

WHAT DO YOU GET WHEN A MONSTER STEPS ON A HOUSE?

Now arrange the circled letters to form the surprise answer, as suggested by the above cartoon.

Print answer here   " ◯◯◯◯◯◯ ◯◯◯◯◯ "

JUMBLE®

Unscramble these four Jumbles, one letter to each square, to form four ordinary words.

LEWJE

PLIMB

GINRAD

UNPOCE

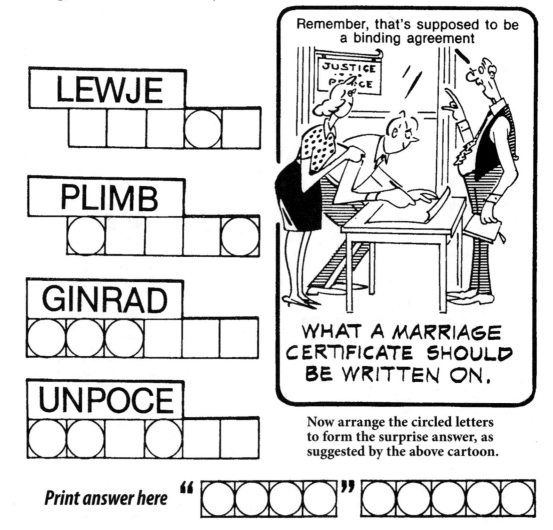

Remember, that's supposed to be a binding agreement

JUSTICE PEACE

WHAT A MARRIAGE CERTIFICATE SHOULD BE WRITTEN ON.

Now arrange the circled letters to form the surprise answer, as suggested by the above cartoon.

Print answer here " ⬭⬭⬭⬭⬭ " ⬭⬭⬭⬭⬭

JUMBLE®

Unscramble these four Jumbles, one letter
to each square, to form four ordinary words.

KAYLE

LURBY

YEUFLE

INVOIS

Freshly
caught

WHAT WERE THE
SHOEMAKER'S TWO
FAVORITE KINDS
OF FISH?

Now arrange the circled letters
to form the surprise answer, as
suggested by the above cartoon.

Print answer here ◯◯◯◯ & ' ◯◯◯

JUMBLE®

Unscramble these four Jumbles, one letter
to each square, to form four ordinary words.

ZYCAR

EMARK

SETTAL

HESTOO

No ambition

And look at those shoes

WHAT LOAFERS LACK.

Now arrange the circled letters
to form the surprise answer, as
suggested by the above cartoon.

Print answer here

JUMBLE®

Unscramble these four Jumbles, one letter to each square, to form four ordinary words.

KERYP

SRIVO

YNERDT

LUBDOE

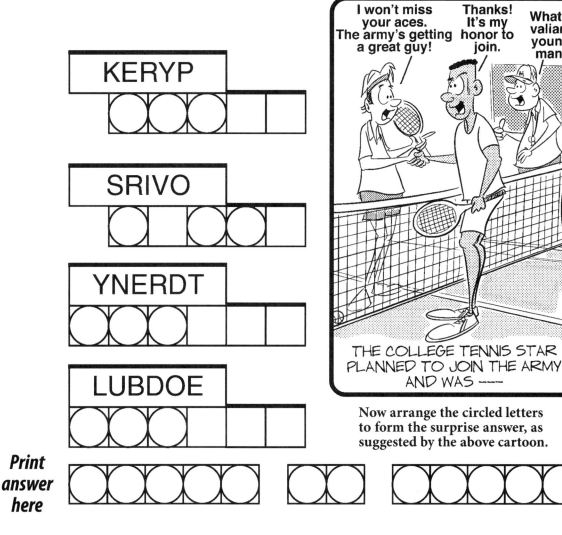

I won't miss your aces. The army's getting a great guy!

Thanks! It's my honor to join.

What a valiant young man.

THE COLLEGE TENNIS STAR PLANNED TO JOIN THE ARMY AND WAS ----

Now arrange the circled letters to form the surprise answer, as suggested by the above cartoon.

Print answer here

JUMBLE®

Unscramble these four Jumbles, one letter to each square, to form four ordinary words.

PROEA

DESYE

RILAPS

SUREVS

What took you so long? Regan's getting worse.

Evidently, the diocese missed some car payments. I had to take a taxi.

TAXI

HE WAS LATE FOR THE EXORCISM BECAUSE HIS CAR HAD BEEN ---

Now arrange the circled letters to form the surprise answer, as suggested by the above cartoon.

Print answer here

JUMBLE®

Unscramble these four Jumbles, one letter to each square, to form four ordinary words.

NIHKT

EOMSO

OTNINO

TREWET

I hate to brag, but the Cubs asked me to play the national anthem. I'm kind of a big deal.

All your hot air must help your playing.

POi

THE TRUMPET PLAYER WITH THE BIG EGO WOULD OFTEN ----

Now arrange the circled letters to form the surprise answer, as suggested by the above cartoon.

Print answer here

⬡⬡⬡⬡ HIS ⬡⬡⬡ ⬡⬡⬡⬡

JUMBLE®

Unscramble these four Jumbles, one letter to each square, to form four ordinary words.

FONTE

HALAP

LGGGIE

CHUPIC

You don't even know the difference between Celsius and Fahrenheit.

At least I'm not 10 to 20 degrees off every day.

93° 97°
96°
98° 101°

THE RIVALRY BETWEEN THE WEATHER FORECASTERS WAS ----

Now arrange the circled letters to form the surprise answer, as suggested by the above cartoon.

Print answer here

JUMBLE®

Unscramble these four Jumbles, one letter to each square, to form four ordinary words.

EMACO

NDORF

YEGRES

TCWISH

We capture all the methane gas from your trash and use it to power your homes.

FOR THE STEUBEN COUNTY LANDFILL, CONVERTING TRASH INTO ELECTRICITY WASN'T A ----

Now arrange the circled letters to form the surprise answer, as suggested by the above cartoon.

Print answer here

JUMBLE®

Unscramble these four Jumbles, one letter
to each square, to form four ordinary words.

TIDOT

ATING

SREDYS

DROVEN

BOB'S BODY SHOP

I am so glad to see those dings gone.

We've been pretty busy since that hailstorm.

ONCE HER CAR WAS REPAIRED,
SHE SAID THIS IN REGARD
TO THE DAMAGE ---

Now arrange the circled letters
to form the surprise answer, as
suggested by the above cartoon.

Print
answer
here

"   -   "

JUMBLE ®

Unscramble these four Jumbles, one letter
to each square, to form four ordinary words.

BLACE

RAWEY

GREDDE

PLAWOL

Was the line long?

Yes, but I got here early.

Is that a smile?

WHEN THE CARTOONISTS
SKETCHED PEOPLE IN THE
COMIC SHOP, THEY ———

Now arrange the circled letters
to form the surprise answer, as
suggested by the above cartoon.

Print
answer
here

JUMBLE®

Unscramble these four Jumbles, one letter to each square, to form four ordinary words.

DYIGD

RACKN

FUTEFB

LUTCPS

I'm running out of room for your orders.

I'm trying.

THE SERVER COULDN'T GET THE PANCAKES TO THE TABLES FAST ENOUGH. ORDERS WERE ----

Now arrange the circled letters to form the surprise answer, as suggested by the above cartoon.

Print answer here

JUMBLE.

Unscramble these four Jumbles, one letter to each square, to form four ordinary words.

GRUYB

MIHDU

TONCOY

SHOCCR

I think all the states will love this song.

It is a catchy tune.

"THE STAR-SPANGLED BANNER" BECAME THE NATIONAL ANTHEM IN 1931, MAKING IT ---

Now arrange the circled letters to form the surprise answer, as suggested by the above cartoon.

Print answer here

JUMBLE®

Unscramble these four Jumbles, one letter to each square, to form four ordinary words.

MUYTM

MAIDT

SASNEO

CIPHUC

Do you need any help with the Jumble?

Nope! I don't care if it takes all day. I'm going to solve this.

EVEN WITHOUT A BRAIN, THE SCARECROW COULD DO ANYTHING HE ---

Now arrange the circled letters to form the surprise answer, as suggested by the above cartoon.

Print answer here

JUMBLE®

Unscramble these four Jumbles, one letter to each square, to form four ordinary words.

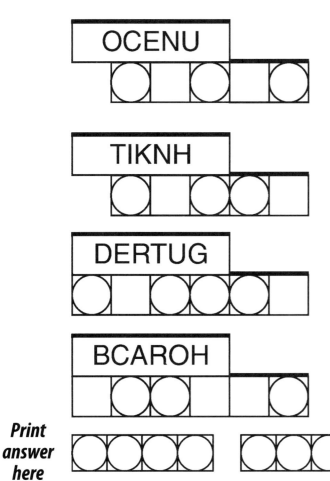

OCENU

TIKNH

DERTUG

BCAROH

I don't know how much longer these will pump out oil.

They'll need to spend money on these rigs.

THE OIL DRILLING BUSINESS WAS FAILING BECAUSE THE OWNERS WERE RUNNING IT ---

Now arrange the circled letters to form the surprise answer, as suggested by the above cartoon.

Print answer here

JUMBLE®

Unscramble these four Jumbles, one letter
to each square, to form four ordinary words.

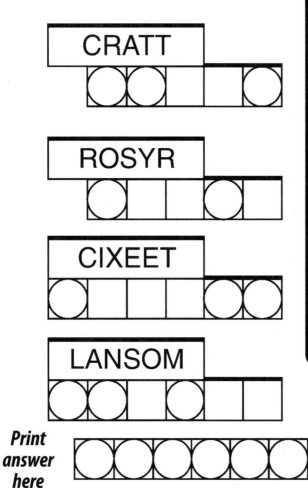

CRATT

ROSYR

CIXEET

LANSOM

The Accademia is around this corner.

Let's take Via de' Pucci to Via Ricasoli and we'll be there.

Via de' Pucci

WITH GPS MAPS ON THEIR NEW PHONES, EVEN TOURISTS CAN BE ---

Now arrange the circled letters
to form the surprise answer, as
suggested by the above cartoon.

*Print
answer
here*

JUMBLE®

Unscramble these four Jumbles, one letter
to each square, to form four ordinary words.

PAAHL

GIBEE

HUSTIA

HNURCB

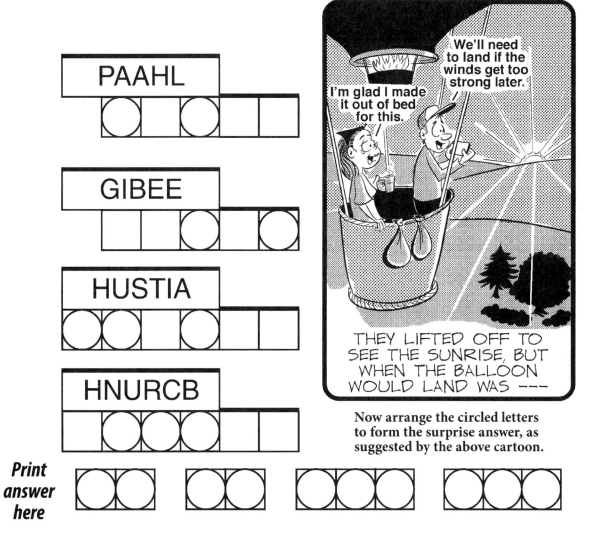

We'll need
to land if the
winds get too
strong later.

I'm glad I made
it out of bed
for this.

THEY LIFTED OFF TO
SEE THE SUNRISE, BUT
WHEN THE BALLOON
WOULD LAND WAS ---

Now arrange the circled letters
to form the surprise answer, as
suggested by the above cartoon.

**Print
answer
here**

JUMBLE®

Unscramble these four Jumbles, one letter to each square, to form four ordinary words.

AADLS

WTRIL

HOPSLI

URAQES

MATT'S LAUNDROMAT

OUT OF BUSINESS

I can't believe I lost everything.

Yep. You're done. Here's my bill.

THE OWNER OF THE FAILED LAUNDROMAT WAS ---

Now arrange the circled letters to form the surprise answer, as suggested by the above cartoon.

Print answer here

JUMBLE®

Unscramble these four Jumbles, one letter to each square, to form four ordinary words.

KELEN

TEHTE

MICTOM

PORRUA

It's you! Hello! How long will I live? Why am I here?

Well, "Hello," to you too.

ANDROIDS DON'T NEED TO DIE TO ---

Now arrange the circled letters to form the surprise answer, as suggested by the above cartoon.

Print answer here

JUMBLE®

Unscramble these four Jumbles, one letter
to each square, to form four ordinary words.

RWONB

OWNOS

CEDDEA

JENRIU

You have such a great family bakery.

It's allowed us to spend time with our kids.

One day we hope to leave it to the children.

THE BAKERY OWNED
BY THE MARRIED
COUPLE HAD TWO ---

Now arrange the circled letters
to form the surprise answer, as
suggested by the above cartoon.

*Print
answer
here*

JUMBLE®

Unscramble these four Jumbles, one letter to each square, to form four ordinary words.

DPAAT

PITYS

SOYMLT

CIRNUH

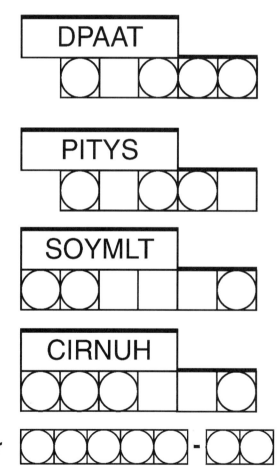

This will engage the engine.

It sure beats this knuckle buster.

TO SELL HIS NEW ELECTRIC IGNITION SYSTEMS, CHARLES F. KETTERING CREATED A ---

Now arrange the circled letters to form the surprise answer, as suggested by the above cartoon.

Print answer here

JUMBLE®

Unscramble these four Jumbles, one letter
to each square, to form four ordinary words.

GINET

WDLOR

GIRHEH

TUFTIO

After you.

I was here first.

HE WAS ABLE TO USE THE
SCALE FIRST BECAUSE
HE HAD THE ---

Now arrange the circled letters
to form the surprise answer, as
suggested by the above cartoon.

Print
answer
here

" "

JUMBLE®

Unscramble these four Jumbles, one letter
to each square, to form four ordinary words.

RIKHE

SACEE

DULCED

YAWONH

Oh, my.
I feel like a
house
landed on
my skull.

I made you a
nice potion to
help.

AFTER A LONG DAY OF
CASTING SINISTER SPELLS,
THE EVIL WITCH HAD A ---

Now arrange the circled letters
to form the surprise answer, as
suggested by the above cartoon.

*Print
answer
here*

JUMBLE®

Unscramble these four Jumbles, one letter
to each square, to form four ordinary words.

PRAAT

FTORN

ROMPIT

DEULHD

All warmed up.
Let's begin!

WHEN THEY SANG
SONGS AT THE SUMMIT,
THEY SANG THEM ----

Now arrange the circled letters
to form the surprise answer, as
suggested by the above cartoon.

Print answer here

JUMBLE®

Unscramble these four Jumbles, one letter to each square, to form four ordinary words.

GAUVE

TOMOT

RNINEW

CROTHO

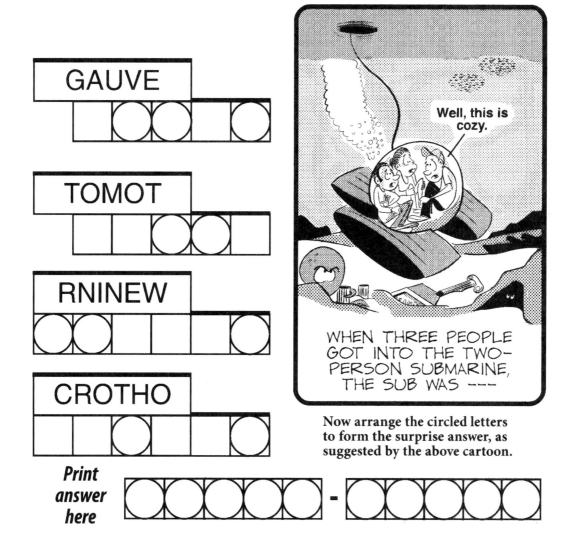

Well, this is cozy.

WHEN THREE PEOPLE GOT INTO THE TWO-PERSON SUBMARINE, THE SUB WAS ---

Now arrange the circled letters to form the surprise answer, as suggested by the above cartoon.

Print answer here

◯◯◯◯◯ - ◯◯◯◯◯

JUMBLE®

Unscramble these four Jumbles, one letter to each square, to form four ordinary words.

FARGT

KENAL

SEWEFT

SWIMOD

Here's my next outfit for you.

I'm not going to put that on. You would never see me in that.

What is it?

THE APPEAL OF BEING A FASHION MODEL WAS ---

Now arrange the circled letters to form the surprise answer, as suggested by the above cartoon.

Print answer here

JUMBLE

Unscramble these four Jumbles, one letter
to each square, to form four ordinary words.

WTYIT

SUMEA

GREVON

MIYFAN

All you got was
chicken for lunch?
Did you get
enough for me?

I sure did. Let's go
eat outside away
from the hair.

TWO BIT
BARBER
SHOP

THE BARBERS LIKED
TO EAT THEIR MEALS
WITHOUT ALL THE ---

Now arrange the circled letters
to form the surprise answer, as
suggested by the above cartoon.

Print answer here

JUMBLE®

Unscramble these four Jumbles, one letter
to each square, to form four ordinary words.

KORPE

PMIBL

BAZAEL

YAASLW

FOR KING KONG,
FINDING CLOTHING
THAT FIT WAS A ---

Now arrange the circled letters
to form the surprise answer, as
suggested by the above cartoon.

Print
answer
here

JUMBLE®

Unscramble these four Jumbles, one letter to each square, to form four ordinary words.

DURED

GYOGS

CLAJAK

SOBPHI

Want to trade places?

Not a chance. I can't believe I get paid to do this.

THE QUALITY CONTROL PERSON AT THE CUSHION FACTORY LIKED HER ---

Now arrange the circled letters to form the surprise answer, as suggested by the above cartoon.

Print answer here

JUMBLE®

Unscramble these four Jumbles, one letter to each square, to form four ordinary words.

FEORF

PERIG

SUUGNF

PAPERA

THE DAILY CATCH

You've got me hooked, but I won't be cooked by you.

I love these guys!

THE FISH THAT STARTED THEIR OWN ROCK BAND WERE ---

Now arrange the circled letters to form the surprise answer, as suggested by the above cartoon.

Print answer here

JUMBLE®

Unscramble these four Jumbles, one letter
to each square, to form four ordinary words.

SPEWT

FINUY

DANURO

CLOYNO

The last one's
in position.

Let's fire
it up!

THE NEW HEATING/COOLING
SYSTEM WOULD BE READY
WHEN THEY HAD ALL THEIR ----

Now arrange the circled letters
to form the surprise answer, as
suggested by the above cartoon.

*Print
answer
here*

" ⃝⃝⃝⃝⃝ " ⃝⃝ ⃝ ⃝⃝⃝

JUMBLE®

Unscramble these four Jumbles, one letter to each square, to form four ordinary words.

WOHNS

RITLF

ZOICRE

LIPYOC

Wow! You're the most gifted angler I've ever seen.

Thanks! Experience helps.

WHEN IT CAME TO CATCHING TROUT, THE SKILLED ANGLER WAS ----

Now arrange the circled letters to form the surprise answer, as suggested by the above cartoon.

Print answer here " ☐☐☐ - ☐☐☐☐ - ☐☐☐☐ "

JUMBLE

Unscramble these four Jumbles, one letter
to each square, to form four ordinary words.

DAAPN

BEFLA

LAVELY

PILUHL

That dog's crazy!
We're out of here.

He doesn't
bother me.
I'm staying.

THE BIRD NEVER GOT
UPSET OR PERTURBED
AND WAS ALWAYS
COMPOSED. HE WAS ---

Now arrange the circled letters
to form the surprise answer, as
suggested by the above cartoon.

Print
answer
here

JUMBLE®

Unscramble these four Jumbles, one letter
to each square, to form four ordinary words.

NIRLE

NECHE

TUACIQ

CICIAD

THE REINDEER ATE THE
GROWTH ON THE TREE
BARK AND WERE ---

This is so good!

I know!

Now arrange the circled letters
to form the surprise answer, as
suggested by the above cartoon.

Print answer here " ⃝⃝⃝⃝⃝⃝ " ⃝⃝

JUMBLE®

Unscramble these four Jumbles, one letter to each square, to form four ordinary words.

LOCRO

VEELL

NASADL

PIBSOY

Thank you, here's your money.

This sure beats a cookie!

Who had red and who had white?

How much?

DRACULA STARTED PAYING FOR PLASMA BECAUSE HE KNEW THAT ---

Now arrange the circled letters to form the surprise answer, as suggested by the above cartoon.

Print answer here

" "

JUMBLE®

Unscramble these four Jumbles, one letter
to each square, to form four ordinary words.

SUGET

BSIRK

GIRDIF

KERBON

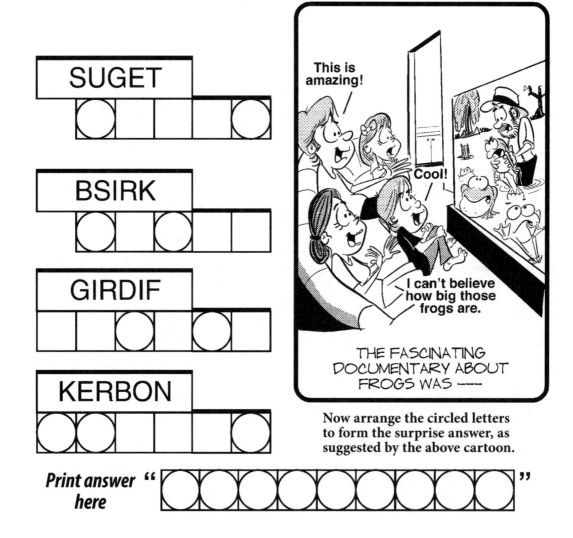

This is amazing!

Cool!

I can't believe how big those frogs are.

THE FASCINATING
DOCUMENTARY ABOUT
FROGS WAS ----

Now arrange the circled letters
to form the surprise answer, as
suggested by the above cartoon.

Print answer "⬭⬭⬭⬭⬭⬭⬭⬭⬭⬭"
here

JUMBLE®

Unscramble these four Jumbles, one letter to each square, to form four ordinary words.

HHCNU

HRTTU

ENGLED

AINAGU

Look! More people.

Morning!

Bonjour.

Don't you love the view from here?

HOW DO THEY SAY HELLO IN THE ALPS?

Now arrange the circled letters to form the surprise answer, as suggested by the above cartoon.

Print answer here " ◯◯◯◯ " ◯◯◯◯◯

JUMBLE®

Unscramble these four Jumbles, one letter to each square, to form four ordinary words.

GADEA

IRCIE

LNUTEN

TERXOP

Another month, another mouth.

I think we're keeping the doctor very busy and well paid.

Ha ha!

WITH SO MUCH DENTAL WORK NEEDED, THEY JOKED ABOUT HAVING AN ORTHODONTIST ---

Now arrange the circled letters to form the surprise answer, as suggested by the above cartoon.

Print answer here

JUMBLE®

Unscramble these four Jumbles, one letter to each square, to form four ordinary words.

LEVTA

LOIOG

ASEWES

CEYPAH

How about a bid of $1,000? How about $500? $100 anyone?

This is for a great cause. Won't anyone bid something?

WHEN NOT ONE PERSON BID IN THE CHARITY AUCTION, THE HOST THOUGHT ---

Now arrange the circled letters to form the surprise answer, as suggested by the above cartoon.

Print answer here

⬡⬡⬡⬡ ⬡⬡⬡⬡⬡ ?

JUMBLE®

Unscramble these four Jumbles, one letter
to each square, to form four ordinary words.

WTISF

STFIH

VATDEN

ZARNBE

I thought you were going to play poker.

I did. I had a pair of kings and bet everything right away and lost.

That was quick.

HE LOST AFTER GOING "ALL IN" AND HAD TO GIVE HIS WIFE THE ---

Now arrange the circled letters to form the surprise answer, as suggested by the above cartoon.

Print answer here

⬡⬡⬡⬡⬡ - ⬡⬡⬡⬡   ⬡⬡⬡⬡

JUMBLE®

Unscramble these four Jumbles, one letter to each square, to form four ordinary words.

VOLNE

EOGGU

WHOGTR

RIDHOA

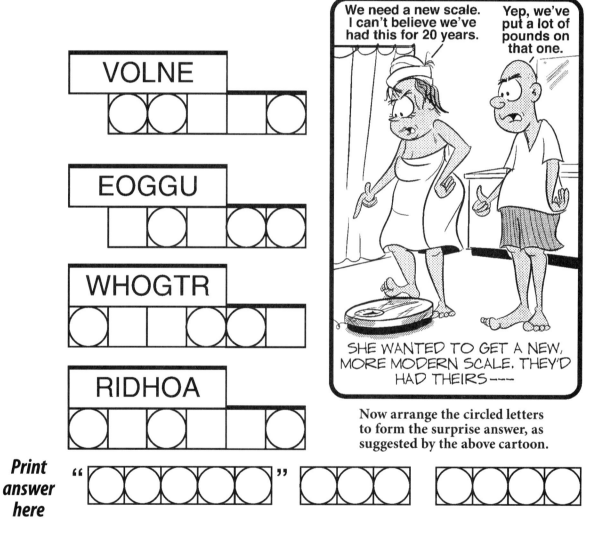

We need a new scale. I can't believe we've had this for 20 years.

Yep, we've put a lot of pounds on that one.

SHE WANTED TO GET A NEW, MORE MODERN SCALE. THEY'D HAD THEIRS ----

Now arrange the circled letters to form the surprise answer, as suggested by the above cartoon.

Print answer here

" ⃝⃝⃝⃝⃝ " ⃝⃝⃝ ⃝⃝⃝⃝

JUMBLE®

Unscramble these four Jumbles, one letter
to each square, to form four ordinary words.

TUYOH

LUPIT

PHOYCP

RANTDS

You distract him,
and I'll swoop in
to scare him.

Great
plan!

WHEN THE OWLS MADE THEIR
PLANS, THEY WERE ---

Now arrange the circled letters
to form the surprise answer, as
suggested by the above cartoon.

**Print answer
here**

JUMBLE®

Unscramble these four Jumbles, one letter to each square, to form four ordinary words.

GWUNS

THUMO

SLCOTY

KAWYEL

Now try putting the north pole into another north pole.

They won't attract.

THEY STUDIED THE ATTRACTIVE PROPERTIES OF CERTAIN METALS AT THE ----

Now arrange the circled letters to form the surprise answer, as suggested by the above cartoon.

Print answer here

JUMBLE®

Unscramble these four Jumbles, one letter
to each square, to form four ordinary words.

EYTSA

SIPEO

GEMAPI

BRFDIO

Big Ben's about to chime at the quarter hour.

According to this, Big Ben is the nickname for the Great Bell of the clock.

BIG BEN RINGS ON A REGULAR BASIS WITH THE ----

Now arrange the circled letters
to form the surprise answer, as
suggested by the above cartoon.

Print
answer
here

JUMBLE®

Unscramble these four Jumbles, one letter to each square, to form four ordinary words.

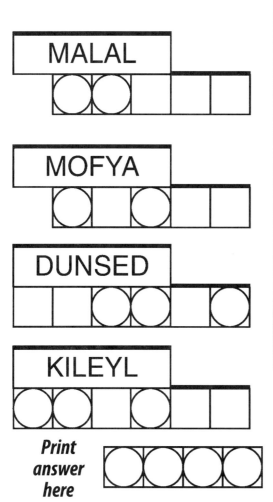

MALAL

MOFYA

DUNSED

KILEYL

No more! We're inundated!

What?

CLOSED

THE GARBAGE DUMP OVERFLOWED WHEN THE ---

Now arrange the circled letters to form the surprise answer, as suggested by the above cartoon.

Print answer here

JUMBLE®

Unscramble these four Jumbles, one letter
to each square, to form four ordinary words.

UHISS

MLURE

GOTOES

HLITFG

THE CONCH SOUP WAS QUITE
EXPENSIVE, BUT CUSTOMERS
WERE HAPPY TO ---

Now arrange the circled letters
to form the surprise answer, as
suggested by the above cartoon.

Print answer here

JUMBLE®

Unscramble these four Jumbles, one letter to each square, to form four ordinary words.

NHYAD

KRIQU

RAFOLV

GEDLEN

I'm going to be late if I have to keep dodging people on the side of the road.

MOST PEOPLE WOULD HAVE HELPED THE STRANDED MOTORIST, BUT HE WASN'T THAT ---

Now arrange the circled letters to form the surprise answer, as suggested by the above cartoon.

Print answer here

JUMBLE®

Unscramble these four Jumbles, one letter
to each square, to form four ordinary words.

BLACE

SAHLS

ARFITF

PLAWOL

Here's the skinny-
we'll be opening up
25 stores this year.

Our
"Diet Dinners"
will be
everywhere.

THE NEW RESTAURANT CHAIN
OFFERED A HEALTHFUL MENU
AT ALL OF THEIR ---

Now arrange the circled letters
to form the surprise answer, as
suggested by the above cartoon.

Print answer here " ◯◯◯ - ◯◯◯◯ "

JUMBLE®

Unscramble these four Jumbles, one letter to each square, to form four ordinary words.

NEEUV

PEDIT

WAYLEK

NAHRGA

It sure beats cobblestones.

The automobile owners love it.

Main First

WHEN ASPHALT BECAME COMMONLY USED ON ROADS, IT ---

Now arrange the circled letters to form the surprise answer, as suggested by the above cartoon.

Print answer here

JUMBLE®

Unscramble these four Jumbles, one letter to each square, to form four ordinary words.

NCULH

WEYNL

FCDAEE

AIPIRM

You're no nurse! You're a guy! Get me a girl nurse!

How 'bout I get you a time machine, and you go back 50 years.

THE NURSE WAS TRYING TO DO HIS JOB, BUT THE PATIENT WAS BEING EXTREMELY ---

Now arrange the circled letters to form the surprise answer, as suggested by the above cartoon.

Print answer here

JUMBLE®

Unscramble these four Jumbles, one letter
to each square, to form four ordinary words.

RAWYE

TOBUD

COTONY

XNEOGY

Right on time.

Here we go.

THE CIRCLES BUILT A
COMMUNITY WITH PUBLIC
TRANSPORTATION SO
THEY COULD ---

Now arrange the circled letters
to form the surprise answer, as
suggested by the above cartoon.

Print
answer
here

JUMBLE®

Unscramble these four Jumbles, one letter
to each square, to form four ordinary words.

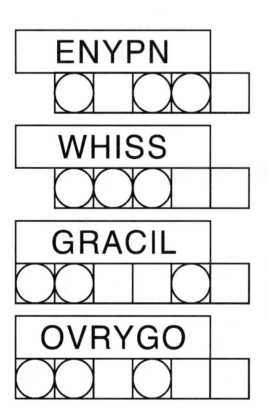

ENYPN

WHISS

GRACIL

OVRYGO

Can someone take these to my car?

We're a little short-handed right now. Honey, can you help?

My back is killing me, but sure.

THE NEW PLANT NURSERY
WAS EXPERIENCING ---

Now arrange the circled letters
to form the surprise answer, as
suggested by the above cartoon.

**Print
answer
here**

JUMBLE®

Unscramble these four Jumbles, one letter to each square, to form four ordinary words.

CAAKB

PMETT

RADYEM

KRHNIS

Introducing the Lincoln penny!

What a great way to honor him.

LINCOLN
PENNY

THE LINCOLN PENNY DEBUTED ON THE CENTENNIAL OF HIS BIRTH BECAUSE ---

Now arrange the circled letters to form the surprise answer, as suggested by the above cartoon.

Print answer here

  "  "

JUMBLE®

Unscramble these four Jumbles, one letter to each square, to form four ordinary words.

BILIA

TIDOT

SLOISF

MRRIPE

This could be the end.

We're in trouble!

WHEN MAGELLAN ROUNDED SOUTH AMERICA HEADED FOR THE PACIFIC, HE WAS IN ---

Now arrange the circled letters to form the surprise answer, as suggested by the above cartoon.

Print answer here

JUMBLE®

Unscramble these four Jumbles, one letter to each square, to form four ordinary words.

ORUDG

VICEH

WYNETT

CTKEHS

So, we all agree. It's time to unionize!

THE GLUE FACTORY EMPLOYEES PLANNED TO START A LABOR UNION AND ---

Now arrange the circled letters to form the surprise answer, as suggested by the above cartoon.

Print answer here

JUMBLE®

Unscramble these four Jumbles, one letter
to each square, to form four ordinary words.

LAVEV

LATYL

CYMLLA

APSYSB

Ms. Jones! I think the waiting room
You're next. became a theater.

I love this
movie!

That's one
way to
get blood.

THE BLOOD DONORS DIDN'T
MIND WAITING, BECAUSE
THE FACILITY HAD A ---

Now arrange the circled letters
to form the surprise answer, as
suggested by the above cartoon.

Print answer here

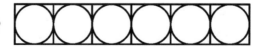

JUMBLE®

Unscramble these four Jumbles, one letter
to each square, to form four ordinary words.

LMIYD

WOSNH

MLEYSL

ATOTOT

No one move.
On three.

THE MOONSHINERS WERE
GETTING THEIR PHOTO
TAKEN SO THEY ---

Now arrange the circled letters
to form the surprise answer, as
suggested by the above cartoon.

*Print
answer
here*

JUMBLE®

Unscramble these four Jumbles, one letter
to each square, to form four ordinary words.

SATYT

TIHPC

TCOEKS

GLONLA

First the Louisiana
Purchase, then the Oregon
Trail. This country keeps
getting bigger.

AMERICA'S WESTWARD
EXPANSION IN THE 1800s
TOOK PLACE ---

Now arrange the circled letters
to form the surprise answer, as
suggested by the above cartoon.

Print answer here ⬡⬡ ⬡⬡⬡⬡⬡⬡

JUMBLE®

Unscramble these four Jumbles, one letter
to each square, to form four ordinary words.

MOBIL

FNTEO

ONIEID

PROTYH

... Two roads diverged in a wood, and I— I took the one less traveled by, And that has made all the difference.

How beautiful!

WHILE STROLLING WITH A FRIEND, ROBERT FROST RECITED HIS NEW COMPOSITION. IT WAS ---

Now arrange the circled letters
to form the surprise answer, as
suggested by the above cartoon.

**Print
answer
here**

JUMBLE®

Unscramble these four Jumbles, one letter
to each square, to form four ordinary words.

ORLED

HNYIS

TRUMET

AAABCN

THE TV NEWSCASTERS
REPORTED THE NEWS FROM
WHERE THEY WERE ---

Now arrange the circled letters
to form the surprise answer, as
suggested by the above cartoon.

**Print answer
here**

JUMBLE®

Unscramble these four Jumbles, one letter to each square, to form four ordinary words.

PUYPG

GUGOE

STIMIF

GRETTA

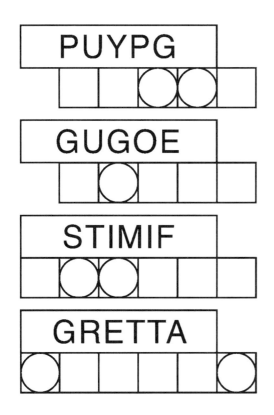

I can get pretty sweaty driving 500 miles.

We can't see the logo.

Cut! Tony, take a break.

THE RACE CAR DRIVER HAD HIS OWN LINE OF DEODORANT CALLED ---

Now arrange the circled letters to form the surprise answer, as suggested by the above cartoon.

Print answer here

JUMBLE®

Unscramble these four Jumbles, one letter
to each square, to form four ordinary words.

DXUEE

KNEAT

GWIJAS

NSDALI

It's like this every year.

I don't know if we can get this done by midnight. I'm exhausted.

FILLING IN ALL THE INFORMATION
ON THE INTERNAL REVENUE
SERVICE FORMS WAS ---

Now arrange the circled letters
to form the surprise answer, as
suggested by the above cartoon.

Print answer here

JUMBLE®

Unscramble these four Jumbles, one letter to each square, to form four ordinary words.

VUMEA

PLEOE

GOACCN

PLOJYA

Look! We've got everything on you. Tell us the truth!

We know you're guilty!

I'm not saying anything more.

THE FBI AGENTS WANTED THE MONEY LAUNDERER TO ---

Now arrange the circled letters to form the surprise answer, as suggested by the above cartoon.

Print answer here

JUMBLE®

Unscramble these four Jumbles, one letter
to each square, to form four ordinary words.

SHRAB

DRYAT

MNYZEE

ASPMUC

I think I saw
something jump
right about there.

We need to get the
chorus out here
with us.

THE STAGE ACTORS WHO
LIKED TO GO FISHING
TOGETHER WERE ---

Now arrange the circled letters
to form the surprise answer, as
suggested by the above cartoon.

*Print
answer
here*

JUMBLE®

Unscramble these four Jumbles, one letter to each square, to form four ordinary words.

CHAYT

EHNSE

AMMHYE

CAYPFI

You must really like these, Mom.
I don't like orange food.
You used my mother's recipe.
No wonder they're so sweet.

WHEN ASKED IF SHE WAS ENJOYING THE SWEET POTATOES, SHE SAID ---

Now arrange the circled letters to form the surprise answer, as suggested by the above cartoon.

Print answer here ◯◯◯ , ◯ " ◯◯◯ "

JUMBLE®

Unscramble these four Jumbles, one letter to each square, to form four ordinary words.

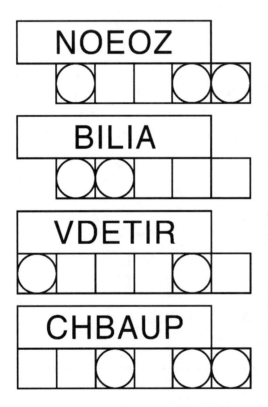

NOEOZ

BILIA

VDETIR

CHBAUP

Hughes is at the door.

How is he going to get that in the air?

HOWARD HUGHES BUILT THE "SPRUCE GOOSE" OUT OF WOOD AND WAS ABLE TO ---

Now arrange the circled letters to form the surprise answer, as suggested by the above cartoon.

Print answer here

 THE

JUMBLE®

Unscramble these four Jumbles, one letter
to each square, to form four ordinary words.

YORFE

DEBIA

GITAMS

FISYHT

WELCOME TO
Reykjavík

Is the J silent?

I never pronounce it the same way twice.

CAN MOST PEOPLE
CORRECTLY PRONOUNCE THE
NAME OF ICELAND'S CAPITAL?

Now arrange the circled letters
to form the surprise answer, as
suggested by the above cartoon.

Print
answer
here

◯◯'◯ ◯◯◯◯ ◯◯ ◯◯◯

JUMBLE®

Unscramble these four Jumbles, one letter
to each square, to form four ordinary words.

MAFER

GSRUH

NHUBCR

POYCML

WHEN BOTH DOGS WENT
AFTER THE BALL AT THE SAME
TIME, THE BALL WAS ---

Now arrange the circled letters
to form the surprise answer, as
suggested by the above cartoon.

Print
answer
here

JUMBLE®

Unscramble these four Jumbles, one letter
to each square, to form four ordinary words.

GYROL

PIENT

LTEERN

DRROBE

No crossing
without paying
two gold pieces
apiece.

Forget it,
you old
grump! We'll
walk around.

THE FOLKLORE CHARACTERS
WANTED TO CROSS THE RIVER
BUT DIDN'T WANT TO USE THE ---

Now arrange the circled letters
to form the surprise answer, as
suggested by the above cartoon.

*Print
answer
here*

JUMBLE®

Unscramble these four Jumbles, one letter
to each square, to form four ordinary words.

NAAGI

HNWIC

RILEDD

TRWHAT

This will keep things sterile.

Golly! And you can still use your fingers!

REGARDING THE INVENTION OF LATEX SURGICAL GLOVES IN 1894, WILLIAM HALSTEAD ---

Now arrange the circled letters
to form the surprise answer, as
suggested by the above cartoon.

**Print
answer
here**

JUMBLE®

Unscramble these four Jumbles, one letter to each square, to form four ordinary words.

TURTE

NEESS

GSITTH

BIBRAT

You gave me my first headache.

No one knows your moves like I do.

THE RAM FRIENDS, WHO LOVED TO SMASH THEIR HEADS TOGETHER, WERE ---

Now arrange the circled letters to form the surprise answer, as suggested by the above cartoon.

Print answer here

" "

JUMBLE®

Unscramble these four Jumbles, one letter
to each square, to form four ordinary words.

KENAL

GRTIE

LMINEB

HYSECP

WHEN SCIENTIST
ALBERT GHIORSO
ADDED TO THE PERIODIC
TABLE, HE WAS ---

Now arrange the circled letters
to form the surprise answer, as
suggested by the above cartoon.

**Print
answer
here**

JUMBLE®

Unscramble these four Jumbles, one letter
to each square, to form four ordinary words.

GHIST

PTYIS

OMHOTS

RPEATI

I thought I measured this twice.

I told you the risers are seven-and-a-half inches!

THE CONSTRUCTION OF THE
STAIRCASE WASN'T GOING
WELL BECAUSE OF ALL THE ---

Now arrange the circled letters
to form the surprise answer, as
suggested by the above cartoon.

Print answer here

JUMBLE®

Unscramble these four Jumbles, one letter
to each square, to form four ordinary words.

MISYL

DUGEN

CIDPET

RANSIP

I don't mind that he didn't even notice me! It's always fun just trying.

THE RAIN MADE IT HARD FOR THE GHOST TO HAUNT PEOPLE, BUT IT DIDN'T ---

Now arrange the circled letters
to form the surprise answer, as
suggested by the above cartoon.

Print
answer
here

 HIS

JUMBLE®

Unscramble these four Jumbles, one letter to each square, to form four ordinary words.

BORUT

GARWE

DPLUED

YEONRR

We're almost there.

THE BOTTOM OF THE VALLEY WAS A LITTLE FURTHER ---

Now arrange the circled letters to form the surprise answer, as suggested by the above cartoon.

Print answer here

◯◯◯◯ THE ◯◯◯◯

JUMBLE®

Unscramble these four Jumbles, one letter
to each square, to form four ordinary words.

LSSOH

DICEH

RALLUP

CASCUT

How
convenient.

It all goes
down the
drain.

SHE LOVED HAVING THE
NEW WAY OF DISCARDING
FOOD SCRAPS IN THE SINK ---

Now arrange the circled letters
to form the surprise answer, as
suggested by the above cartoon.

Print
answer
here

JUMBLE®

Unscramble these four Jumbles, one letter to each square, to form four ordinary words.

MEASU

NRDIG

TRYOHN

ZEFEER

Hey! I thought you were staying with this diet.

I'm done! I'm starving! I'll take a Big Kahuna Burger.

Coming right up.

SHE TRIED NOT EATING FOR A FEW DAYS TO LOSE WEIGHT, BUT FOR HER, IT COULDN'T ---

Now arrange the circled letters to form the surprise answer, as suggested by the above cartoon.

Print answer here

JUMBLE®

Unscramble these four Jumbles, one letter to each square, to form four ordinary words.

BLIOM

COUNE

SLUENS

STRAHH

This reminds me of when we first became fromagers.

All our cheeses stunk, in a good way.

THE FRENCH CHEESE MAKERS WERE ALWAYS HAPPY TO TAKE TIME TO ---

Now arrange the circled letters to form the surprise answer, as suggested by the above cartoon.

Print answer here ⬡⬡⬡⬡⬡⬡ THE " ⬡⬡⬡⬡⬡ "

JUMBLE®

Unscramble these four Jumbles, one letter to each square, to form four ordinary words.

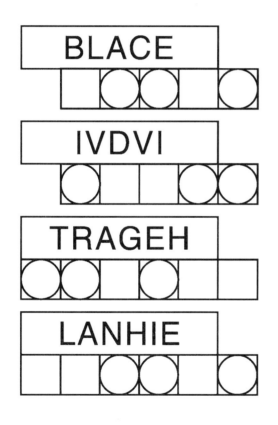

BLACE

IVDVI

TRAGEH

LANHIE

Being the first president, I really should be larger. But people see me first anyway.

I thought you didn't lie.

Lighten up, George.

Bully!

IF GEORGE WASHINGTON'S MOUNT RUSHMORE CARVING CAME TO LIFE, HE'D ---

Now arrange the circled letters to form the surprise answer, as suggested by the above cartoon.

Print answer here

JUMBLE®

Unscramble these four Jumbles, one letter
to each square, to form four ordinary words.

LEOLC

CAKKN

FRATCY

TUREMT

These seem dull. I'll put them in the rejection pile.

Does this count against me?

THE PAIR OF SCISSORS WAS DEFECTIVE AND DIDN'T ---

Now arrange the circled letters
to form the surprise answer, as
suggested by the above cartoon.

Print answer here ◯◯◯◯ **THE** ◯◯◯

JUMBLE®

Unscramble these four Jumbles, one letter to each square, to form four ordinary words.

CRYEM

PIYNP

OJSUYO

RLAMEV

SHE WAS LEARNING
SYNONYMS FOR "LARGE,"
AND LOVED IT ---

Now arrange the circled letters to form the surprise answer, as suggested by the above cartoon.

Print answer here

JUMBLE®

Unscramble these four Jumbles, one letter to each square, to form four ordinary words.

GIGNO

CUHNB

TIRREE

LHIMUE

What'll you have?

I'm glad they parked here.

I'm starving! Let me have a large Cuban!

Me too.

EL JEFE

Cuban sandwich $8
grilled cheese $4
Ham and cheese $7

THE FOOD TRUCK PARKED ALONG THE SIDE OF THE ROAD WAS ABLE TO ---

Now arrange the circled letters to form the surprise answer, as suggested by the above cartoon.

Print answer here

JUMBLE®

Unscramble these four Jumbles, one letter to each square, to form four ordinary words.

PHIOP

YNOEH

GIFTHR

CCSOUT

I really think the colors shine more here.

I think the matte picture is just as good.

THE DIFFICULT DECISION BETWEEN GOING WITH GLOSSY OR MATTE PRINTS WAS A ---

Now arrange the circled letters to form the surprise answer, as suggested by the above cartoon.

Print answer here

JUMBLE®

Unscramble these four Jumbles, one letter to each square, to form four ordinary words.

IDGLU

SEROA

SOIANC

ARPLIS

This has 39 grams of sugar!

That's more than seven teaspoons and 150 calories.

Darn it! One more thing for me to avoid.

WHEN SHE FOUND OUT HOW MANY CALORIES WERE IN HER CAN OF COLA, IT WAS ---

Now arrange the circled letters to form the surprise answer, as suggested by the above cartoon.

Print answer here

"◯◯◯◯◯-◯◯◯◯◯◯◯◯◯"

JUMBLE® Health

Challenger Puzzles

JUMBLE®

Unscramble these six Jumbles, one letter to each square, to form six ordinary words.

LOTTEB

TAULOW

IVIDDE

DELABE

YILSAM

FUNCED

WHAT A BELLY DANCER CAN BE EXPECTED TO DO.

Now arrange the circled letters to form the surprise answer, as suggested by the above cartoon.

Print answer here

⏣⏣⏣⏣⏣⏣⏣ HER ⏣⏣⏣⏣⏣⏣

JUMBLE

Unscramble these six Jumbles, one letter
to each square, to form six ordinary words.

UNBOYT

MIULEH

BABRYC

SOLANG

REKALT

TAPHAY

MAY I INTRODUCE YOU
TO MY HUSBAND?

Now arrange the circled letters
to form the surprise answer, as
suggested by the above cartoon.

Print answer here

" ☐☐☐☐ " ☐ A ☐☐☐ OF ☐☐☐☐ "

JUMBLE

Unscramble these six Jumbles, one letter
to each square, to form six ordinary words.

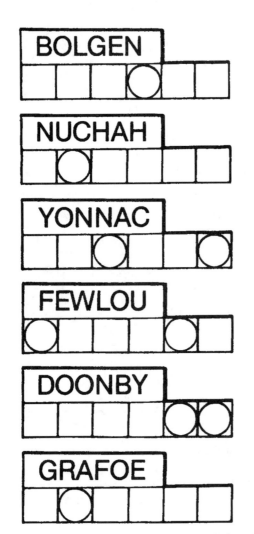

BOLGEN

NUCHAH

YONNAC

FEWLOU

DOONBY

GRAFOE

WHY YOU SHOULD
GET UP BEFORE
DAYLIGHT WHEN YOU'RE
TRYING TO FIND THE
ANSWER TO A
TOUGH PROBLEM.

Now arrange the circled letters
to form the surprise answer, as
suggested by the above cartoon.

Print answer here

IT'LL
SOON

JUMBLE®

Unscramble these six Jumbles, one letter
to each square, to form six ordinary words.

CIVONE

FALOTA

INGRYT

TEWPER

NORMAT

CHARNB

BAKER'

YOU SHOULD TAKE
A NUMBER AT THAT
POPULAR PASTRY
SHOP IN ORDER TO
KEEP THIS.

Now arrange the circled letters
to form the surprise answer, as
suggested by the above cartoon.

Print answer here

YOUR " ☐☐☐☐ " UNDER ☐☐☐☐☐☐☐☐

JUMBLE®

Unscramble these six Jumbles, one letter to each square, to form six ordinary words.

STELEN

LAYGEL

HUTORF

MICOPY

REBLUT

THECCI

COULD THIS BE
ANOTHER NAME FOR
ALL THE MAIL THAT'S
ON ITS WAY TO
THOSE CONGRESSMEN?

Now arrange the circled letters to form the surprise answer, as suggested by the above cartoon.

Print answer here

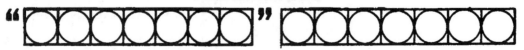

JUMBLE

Unscramble these six Jumbles, one letter to each square, to form six ordinary words.

ROOVED

APHERM

LARNAC

ORMMEY

MURBEN

INGOPE

WHAT THE BOY SCOUT SAID WHEN HE FIXED THE HORN ON THE LITTLE OLD LADY'S BICYCLE.

Now arrange the circled letters to form the surprise answer, as suggested by the above cartoon.

Print answer here

" ⬡⬡⬡⬡ ⬡⬡⬡⬡⬡⬡⬡⬡⬡ "

JUMBLE®

Unscramble these six Jumbles, one letter to each square, to form six ordinary words.

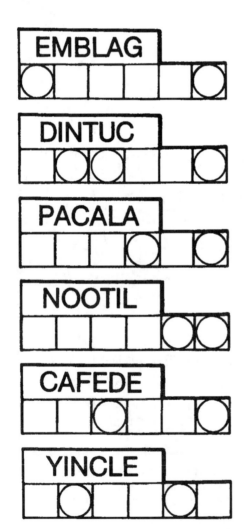

EMBLAG

DINTUC

PACALA

NOOTIL

CAFEDE

YINCLE

Always boasting

NOTHING GETS A PERSON ALL UP IN THE AIR QUICKER THAN THIS.

Now arrange the circled letters to form the surprise answer, as suggested by the above cartoon.

Print answer here

JUMBLE®

Unscramble these six Jumbles, one letter to each square, to form six ordinary words.

LOMOGY

VORCLE

NIVERM

BLOGIE

EATREA

YEWARL

Brr-it's cold in here

THAT ANCIENT STATUE PHONED HIS INSURANCE BROKER BECAUSE HE NEEDED THIS.

Now arrange the circled letters to form the surprise answer, as suggested by the above cartoon.

Print answer here

" "

JUMBLE®

Unscramble these six Jumbles, one letter to each square, to form six ordinary words.

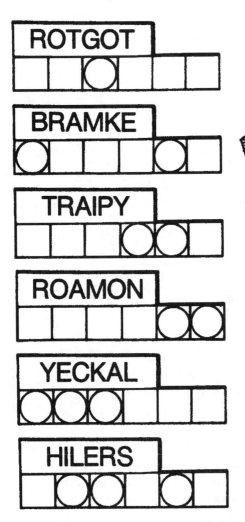

ROTGOT

BRAMKE

TRAIPY

ROAMON

YECKAL

HILERS

Here's a nickel, nephew--spend it wisely

WHAT THE STINGY RICH UNCLE WAS.

Now arrange the circled letters to form the surprise answer, as suggested by the above cartoon.

Print answer here

A " ⬡⬡⬡⬡⬡ " ⬡⬡⬡⬡⬡⬡⬡⬡⬡

JUMBLE®

Unscramble these six Jumbles, one letter to each square, to form six ordinary words.

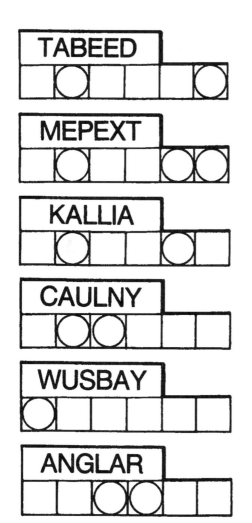

TABEED

MEPEXT

KALLIA

CAULNY

WUSBAY

ANGLAR

Congratulations--you just won the lottery!

He's making it up

THAT PRACTICAL JOKER SHAKES YOUR HAND ONE MINUTE AND ---

Now arrange the circled letters to form the surprise answer, as suggested by the above cartoon.

Print answer here

⬡⬡⬡⬡⬡ YOUR ⬡⬡⬡ THE ⬡⬡⬡⬡

JUMBLE®

Unscramble these six Jumbles, one letter to each square, to form six ordinary words.

INMALY

DOMECY

TRUBET

KOYDEN

AKCEPT

YORTHE

HOW THE OTHER ANIMALS EXPRESSED THEIR RESPECT FOR THE GIRAFFE.

Now arrange the circled letters to form the surprise answer, as suggested by the above cartoon.

Print answer here

THEY ☐☐☐☐☐☐ ☐☐ TO ☐☐☐

JUMBLE®

Unscramble these six Jumbles, one letter
to each square, to form six ordinary words.

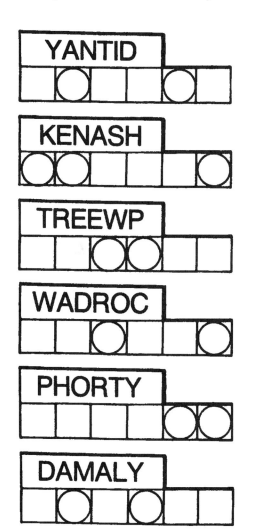

YANTID

KENASH

TREEWP

WADROC

PHORTY

DAMALY

Half the time he was headed
in the wrong direction

ALTHOUGH HE KNEW
HIS JOB "BACKWARDS
AND FORWARDS," HE
WAS FIRED.

Now arrange the circled letters
to form the surprise answer, as
suggested by the above cartoon.

Print answer here

JUMBLE®

Unscramble these six Jumbles, one letter to each square, to form six ordinary words.

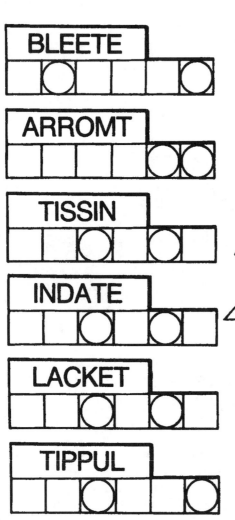

BLEETE

ARROMT

TISSIN

INDATE

LACKET

TIPPUL

HAVE YOU FOUND OUT THE SOURCE OF THAT MOONSHINE YET?

Now arrange the circled letters to form the surprise answer, as suggested by the above cartoon.

Print answer here

" IT'S ⬡ ⬡⬡⬡⬡⬡ ⬡⬡⬡⬡⬡ "

JUMBLE®

Unscramble these six Jumbles, one letter to each square, to form six ordinary words.

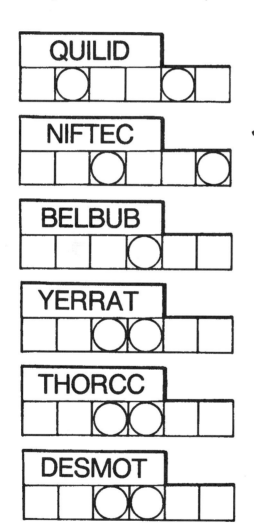

QUILID

NIFTEC

BELBUB

YERRAT

THORCC

DESMOT

I'm going to propose this very minute!

WHEN HE SAW THE WOMAN OF HIS DREAMS, HE WAS THIS.

Now arrange the circled letters to form the surprise answer, as suggested by the above cartoon.

Print answer here

◯◯◯ ◯◯ ◯◯ "◯◯◯◯"

JUMBLE®

Unscramble these six Jumbles, one letter to each square, to form six ordinary words.

LIANEH

LREVAM

GSNROT

RGYGOG

KEVION

FYMNIA

WHEN THEY COLLECTED EASTER EGGS TOGETHER, IT WAS A ---

Now arrange the circled letters to form the surprise answer, as suggested by the above cartoon.

Print answer here

JUMBLE®

Unscramble these six Jumbles, one letter to each square, to form six ordinary words.

HORDSU

FLITLE

PRMYUG

ASYARL

TECOIP

DANECN

When do you put in the aromatics?

You have to wait for the right moment to have the flavors release into the dish.

THE CHEF WAS AT THE POINT IN THE FOOD PREPARATION WHERE IT WAS ---

Now arrange the circled letters to form the surprise answer, as suggested by the above cartoon.

Print answer here

" ⬡⬡⬡⬡⬡ " ⬡⬡⬡ ⬡⬡⬡⬡⬡⬡⬡⬡

JUMBLE®

Unscramble these six Jumbles, one letter
to each square, to form six ordinary words.

HATMFO

INFEED

PUBRAT

KHANES

UALTOW

BULHEM

Now arrange the circled letters
to form the surprise answer, as
suggested by the above cartoon.

Print answer here

JUMBLE®

Unscramble these six Jumbles, one letter to each square, to form six ordinary words.

TNRIGS

LORVET

HEAYMM

TEAHHL

SEDTOD

CELEFE

We all saved our money to buy the necklace you liked so much.

Do you like it, Mom?

I love it! It's priceless, just like all of you!

WHEN HER CHILDREN ALL CHIPPED IN TO BUY HER A GOLD NECKLACE, SHE ---

Now arrange the circled letters to form the surprise answer, as suggested by the above cartoon.

Print answer here

JUMBLE®

Unscramble these six Jumbles, one letter to each square, to form six ordinary words.

VANHEE

TRIBET

KRIQUY

DLUMEO

NROCEF

LWROTE

The terrain and weather make it hard to get to the resources.

We knew that when we purchased it.

ALASKA

EXPLORING ALASKA FOR ITS NATURAL RESOURCES IN THE 1800s WAS DIFFICULT, BUT THAT ---

Now arrange the circled letters to form the surprise answer, as suggested by the above cartoon.

Print answer here

⬡⬡⬡⬡ ⬡⬡⬡⬡ THE ⬡⬡⬡⬡⬡⬡⬡⬡⬡

JUMBLE®

Unscramble these six Jumbles, one letter to each square, to form six ordinary words.

BRAVLE

OFROGT

BYUCON

FNIEEL

MAIDSY

SRWPAL

THE CAR DEALERSHIP PUT UP NEW BILLBOARDS TO ---

Now arrange the circled letters to form the surprise answer, as suggested by the above cartoon.

Print answer here

Answers

1. **Jumbles:** RANCH FAULT HEARSE LIMPID
   Answer: What that precociously bright baby was—
   A FLASH IN THE "PRAM"

2. **Jumbles:** PATIO AFIRE INDIGO FACTOR
   Answer: What the fishing enthusiast was—A "FIN-ATIC"

3. **Jumbles:** WHEAT DIRTY SYSTEM FOSSIL
   Answer: Should a car with automatic drive be entrusted to
   someone who's this?—"SHIFTLESS"

4. **Jumbles:** FUSSY GOURD ADJOIN DISARM
   Answer: What a spoiled brat does—"NO'S" HIS OWN DAD

5. **Jumbles:** SHEAF CLOUT FUMBLE TREATY
   Answer: Horseback riding is a sport that sometimes makes the
   novice feel this—BETTER OFF

6. **Jumbles:** DECAY LIGHT CALMLY BAKERY
   Answer: What there was plenty of after the post office caught
   fire—"BLACK MAIL"

7. **Jumbles:** QUEER FAINT BENIGN TANKER
   Answer: He thinks he's going places when he's really this—
   BEING "TAKEN"

8. **Jumbles:** GUARD HITCH STICKY COSTLY
   Answer: What to say to the man who thinks he can afford a boat
   like that—"YACHTS" OF LUCK

9. **Jumbles:** ACRID FUSSY REALTY TEMPER
   Answer: He wanted to be an astronaut, but they said all he had
   taken up in school was this—"SPACE"

10. **Jumbles:** PIANO TULIP GUILTY PUNDIT
    Answer: A diet is something you keep putting off while you
    keep this—PUTTING ON

11. **Jumbles:** OPERA MOUNT SPONGE HELPER
    Answer: What that tall beachcomber was—
    A LONG "SHOREMAN"

12. **Jumbles:** ICING GUILE SINFUL FORMAL
    Answer: People who go all out often end up this way—ALL IN

13. **Jumbles:** CRUSH UPPER SPRUCE POORLY
    Answer: An elopement sometimes results when man proposes
    and future mother-in-law does this—OPPOSES

14. **Jumbles:** ORBIT APPLY CHARGE BIGAMY
    Answer: Candles on birthday cakes help people make this—
    "LIGHT" OF THEIR AGE

15. **Jumbles:** QUEEN DUSKY BRUTAL SMUDGE
    Answer: How automobiles moved before anyone thought of
    using lubricating oil—THEY JUST SQUEAKED BY

16. **Jumbles:** FLANK VALVE RATHER SUBWAY
    Answer: What's the environment like when you sleep alongside
    your horse?—VERY STABLE

17. **Jumbles:** PECAN GOURD UNTRUE NEPHEW
    Answer: What happened to the restaurant that served those
    substandard submarine sandwiches?—IT WENT UNDER

18. **Jumbles:** GRIME SPURN KENNEL INSIST
    Answer: What the cops looked for when there was a robbery at
    the sausage factory—THE MISSING "LINK"

19. **Jumbles:** GLADE APART COOKIE ENOUGH
    Answer: What those stray dogs enjoyed most at dinnertime—
    "POUND" CAKE

20. **Jumbles:** CABLE GROUP BALSAM FUNGUS
    Answer: What that heroic fireman became—"FLAMOUS"

21. **Jumbles:** EXILE LAPEL PRISON COMPLY
    Answer: What you might find at that mom and pop tire
    shop—A NICE "SPARE"

22. **Jumbles:** ANNOY PLAID WALLOP TWINGE
    Answer: What you might end up with from too much
    housecleaning—A WINDOW "PAIN"

23. **Jumbles:** TRILL GOUGE VACUUM FLEECE
    Answer: What you might do with the menu when you're dining
    at a fish restaurant—"MULLET" OVER

24. **Jumbles:** BRAND FROZE SIZZLE INFECT
    Answer: He went unrecognized when he had this—
    HIS "FEZ" LIFTED

25. **Jumbles:** GAUGE BELIE SCRIBE DAINTY
    Answer: When the price of sugar escalated, the customers did
    this—RAISED "CANE"

26. **Jumbles:** HUMID LOUSE JOCKEY OPIATE
    Answer: How he felt when he finally reached the very top of the
    mountain—"PEAK-ED"

27. **Jumbles:** CHESS FLUTE ALKALI ROSARY
    Answer: What the champion malted milk maker thought he got
    when the boss gave him a bonus—A FAIR "SHAKE"

28. **Jumbles:** PRUNE OLDER VERIFY MORTAR
    Answer: Every time he ran two hundred yards, he actually did
    this — MOVED TWO FEET

29. **Jumbles:** EXCEL INKED GROUCH TOWARD
    Answer: After getting two college diplomas, he led a life of
    crime until the cops threatened him with this—A THIRD DEGREE

30. **Jumbles:** DOUBT TYPED SINGLE PURITY
    Answer: The only way to learn the coffee business—
    FROM THE "GROUNDS" UP

31. **Jumbles:** FIFTY GORGE ENDURE ARCTIC
    Answer: Retreads are sold for people who want to do this—
    "RE-TIRE"

32. **Jumbles:** ABOVE BRAIN FELLOW ARTFUL
    Answer: When you buy a herd of bison, you can expect to
    receive this—A BUFFALO "BILL"

33. **Jumbles:** TRIPE CROWN FROSTY PAUNCH
    Answer: What they served in that restaurant favored by the
    karate crowd—"CHOPS"

34. **Jumbles:** MOLDY FEIGN BLAZER NEEDLE
    Answer: That friendly neighborhood bank catered to people
    who were this—"LOAN-LY"

35. **Jumbles:** CAPON TWINE WIZARD MOSQUE
    Answer: Why pillows are so expensive—DOWN IS UP

36. **Jumbles:** MOUSE TASTY LEDGER PRIMER
    Answer: What they were awarded at the graduation ceremonies
    at diving school—"DEEP-LOMAS"

37. **Jumbles:** ENJOY PRIME SPLICE THORAX
    Answer: Is this the best lubricant for furniture wheels?—
    "CASTER" OIL

38. **Jumbles:** SIEGE WHOSE BOUGHT POTENT
    Answer: The smoothest running thing about that car—
    HIS TONGUE

39. **Jumbles:** SHOWY AROMA NIPPLE FALLEN
    Answer: Another name for chivalry—"MALE" POLISH

40. **Jumbles:** FRUIT TOKEN CACTUS LIZARD
    Answer: What's missing from most hot disputes?—COLD FACTS

41. **Jumbles:** CRESS GULLY DENTAL BANNER
    Answer: What the dynamiters' annual shindig was—
    A REAL BLAST

42. **Jumbles:** CHEEK NOBLE BESTOW INVADE
    Answer: Another thing that people are always spilling—
    THE BEANS

43. **Jumbles:** SNACK BOOTY POETIC CARBON
    Answer: That husband and wife knew each other like a book—
    A SCRAP BOOK

44. **Jumbles:** FLUKE AGATE THWART SHOULD
    Answer: Something one's in when one's not in anything else—
    THE ALTOGETHER

45. **Jumbles:** COLIC BRAWL MANAGE ABSORB
    Answer: What building that big tunnel must have been—
    A BIG "BORE"

46. **Jumbles:** JERKY FORGO INWARD ABUSED
Answer: The selfish farmhand had trouble milking the cow, because he had no regard for the feeling of this—"UDDERS" (others)

47. **Jumbles:** ROUSE PLAIT SIPHON ALWAYS
Answer: How to mail an umbrella—BY "PARASOL" POST

48. **Jumbles:** BRINY GAUZE PURPLE DECENT
Answer: The diary is the book where all her secrets are this—"PENNED" UP

49. **Jumbles:** ELEGY HOBBY UPSHOT GUIDED
Answer: What the ant did when he saw the anteater—BUGGED OUT

50. **Jumbles:** LADLE PROXY AUBURN CATCHY
Answer: Some sailors who make their living on water seldom do this—TOUCH IT ON LAND

51. **Jumbles:** ONION BERET UNLOCK HANGER
Answer: Her choice of husband showed better taste than this—HER COOKING

52. **Jumbles:** EVOKE DRAWL WEAPON ARTERY
Answer: Her strong will dominated this—HIS WEAK "WON'T"

53. **Jumbles:** ANISE DAISY BELIEF FAMOUS
Answer: Women use perfume because some men are easily this—LED BY THE NOSE

54. **Jumbles:** KNACK LEECH QUENCH BEDBUG
Answer: Patent medicines were seldom what they were this—"QUACKED" UP TO BE

55. **Jumbles:** PATCHY NIPPY FROZEN ANYONE
Answer: The weather bureau might sometimes be described as this kind of an agency—"NON-PROPHET"

56. **Jumbles:** FEINT AGING GARBLE TANGLE
Answer: In a politician, the gift of gab is often connected with this—THE GIFT OF GRAB

57. **Jumbles:** BOUGH TACKY AWEIGH CROUCH
Answer: What a man actually eats when he swallows his pride—"CROW"

58. **Jumbles:** COWER BLAZE WIDEST FACIAL
Answer: In Wall Street, so-called "good buys" sometimes turn out to be this—FAREWELLS

59. **Jumbles:** CHAFE DANDY MILDEW PAGODA
Answer: A complaint that usually comes from sour grapes—A "WHINE"

60. **Jumbles:** DAUNT HAVOC ASSAIL LEGACY
Answer: There would be fewer cases of love at first sight, if there were more people gifted with this—SECOND SIGHT

61. **Jumbles:** HAIRY MINOR WEDGED FINITE
Answer: What that bathing beauty was worth—"WADING" FOR

62. **Jumbles:** PEONY MOURN BEYOND PUZZLE
Answer: If you watch too much football, you might wear out this—YOUR "END" ZONE

63. **Jumbles:** ESSAY POPPY ROTATE SNAPPY
Answer: A woman may be the reason why a man supposes he does this—PROPOSES

64. **Jumbles:** QUOTA TRUTH GRUBBY CEMENT
Answer: What the roulette wheel took for a change—A TURN FOR THE "BETTOR"

65. **Jumbles:** JUDGE CHIME EXTENT ADVICE
Answer: What happened when four couples went to a restaurant?—EIGHT ATE

66. **Jumbles:** BROIL JUICE EULOGY BAMBOO
Answer: What little whales like best—"BLUBBER" GUM

67. **Jumbles:** BROOD MIRTH OUTLAW TRICKY
Answer: What they called the hardware store's cat—THE "TOOL KIT"

68. **Jumbles:** COMET WEIGH YEOMAN TAUGHT
Answer: Why the cook hurried to the herb garden—HE HADN'T MUCH "THYME" (time)

69. **Jumbles:** SUEDE HANDY PALACE BEFORE
Answer: What the intelligence agent had when he stayed home from work—A "CODE" IN THE HEAD

70. **Jumbles:** BLOAT EMPTY PARISH IMPOSE
Answer: What the tree that everyone gathered under was called—"POP'LAR" (popular)

71. **Jumbles:** HEAVY YOUTH TUSSLE DISOWN
Answer: His aptitude for platitude creates this in his audience—LASSITUDE

72. **Jumbles:** ARMOR NOTCH TALLOW MEDLEY
Answer: Women detest flattery, especially when it's directed towards this—OTHER WOMEN

73. **Jumbles:** HAZEL LIMBO ACTUAL RENDER
Answer: A fire sale is a place where bargain hunters might get this—"BURNED"

74. **Jumbles:** JUMBO TOXIC SCORCH PIRACY
Answer: Something often found in newspapers and on beaches—A COMIC "STRIP"

75. **Jumbles:** FATAL DIZZY INFORM PITIED
Answer: A surgeon might have to cut out something because the patient this—DID NOT

76. **Jumbles:** MANLY BILGE FLAXEN CASKET
Answer: Most people are put out when they're this—"TAKEN IN"

77. **Jumbles:** VENOM MESSY SHREWD OUTLET
Answer: What do you get when a monster steps on a house?—"MUSHED ROOMS"

78. **Jumbles:** JEWEL BLIMP DARING POUNCE
Answer: What a marriage certificate should be written on—"BOND" PAPER

79. **Jumbles:** LEAKY BURLY EYEFUL VISION
Answer: What were the shoemaker's two favorite kinds of fish?—SOLE & 'EEL (heel)

80. **Jumbles:** CRAZY MAKER LATEST SOOTHE
Answer: What loafers lack—SHOELACES

81. **Jumbles:** PERKY VISOR TRENDY DOUBLE
Answer: The college tennis star planned to join the Army and was—PROUD TO SERVE

82. **Jumbles:** OPERA SEEDY SPIRAL VERSUS
Answer: He was late for the exorcism because his car had been—REPOSSESSED

83. **Jumbles:** THINK MOOSE NOTION WETTER
Answer: The trumpet player with the big ego would often—TOOT HIS OWN HORN

84. **Jumbles:** OFTEN ALPHA GIGGLE HICCUP
Answer: The rivalry between the weather forecasters was—HEATING UP

85. **Jumbles:** CAMEO FROND GEYSER SWITCH
Answer: For the Steuben County Landfill, converting trash into electricity wasn't a—WASTE OF ENERGY

86. **Jumbles:** DITTO GIANT DRESSY VENDOR
Answer: Once her car was repaired she said this in regard to the damage—GOOD "RID-DENTS"

87. **Jumbles:** CABLE WEARY DREDGE WALLOP
Answer: When the cartoonists sketched people in the comic shop, they—DREW A CROWD

88. **Jumbles:** GIDDY CRANK BUFFET SCULPT
Answer: The server couldn't get the pancakes to the tables fast enough. Orders were—STACKING UP

89. **Jumbles:** RUGBY HUMID TYCOON SCORCH
Answer: "The Star-Spangled Banner" became the national anthem in 1931, making it—COUNTRY MUSIC

90. **Jumbles:** TUMMY ADMIT SEASON HICCUP
Answer: Even without a brain, the scarecrow could do anything he—PUT HIS MIND TO

91. **Jumbles:** OUNCE THINK TRUDGE BROACH
Answer: The oil drilling business was failing because the owners were running it—INTO THE GROUND

92. **Jumbles:** TRACT SORRY EXCITE SALMON
Answer: With GPS maps on their new phones, even tourists can be—STREET SMART

93. **Jumbles:** ALPHA BEIGE HIATUS BRUNCH
Answer: They lifted off to see the sunrise, but when the balloon would land was—UP IN THE AIR

94. **Jumbles:** SALAD TWIRL POLISH SQUARE
Answer: The owner of the failed laundromat was—WASHED UP

95. **Jumbles:** KNEEL TEETH COMMIT UPROAR
Answer: Androids don't need to die to—MEET THEIR MAKER

96. **Jumbles:** BROWN SWOON DECADE INJURE
Answer: The bakery owned by the married couple had two—BREAD WINNERS

97. **Jumbles:** ADAPT TIPSY MOSTLY URCHIN
Answer: To sell his new electric ignition systems, Charles F. Kettering created a—START-UP COMPANY

98. **Jumbles:** TINGE WORLD HIGHER OUTFIT
Answer: He was able to use the scale first because he had the—RIGHT OF "WEIGH"

99. **Jumbles:** HIKER CEASE CUDDLE ANYHOW
Answer: After a long day of casting sinister spells, the evil witch had a—WICKED HEADACHE

100. **Jumbles:** APART FRONT IMPORT HUDDLE
Answer: When they sang songs at the summit, they sang them—FROM THE TOP

101. **Jumbles:** VAGUE MOTTO WINNER COHORT
Answer: When three people got into the two-person submarine, the sub was—WATER-TIGHT

102. **Jumbles:** GRAFT ANKLE FEWEST WISDOM
Answer: The appeal of being a fashion model was—WEARING OFF

103. **Jumbles:** WITTY AMUSE GOVERN INFAMY
Answer: The barbers liked to eat their meals without all the—TRIMMINGS

104. **Jumbles:** POKER BLIMP ABLAZE ALWAYS
Answer: For King Kong, finding clothing that fit was a—SIZABLE PROBLEM

105. **Jumbles:** UDDER SOGGY JACKAL BISHOP
Answer: The quality control person at the cushion factory liked her—CUSHY JOB

106. **Jumbles:** OFFER GRIPE FUNGUS APPEAR
Answer: The fish that started their own rock band were—GROUPERS

107. **Jumbles:** SWEPT UNIFY AROUND COLONY
Answer: The new heating/cooling system would be ready when they had all their—"DUCTS" IN A ROW

108. **Jumbles:** SHOWN FLIRT COZIER POLICY
Answer: When it came to catching trout, the skilled angler was—"PRO-FISH-IENT"

109. **Jumbles:** PANDA FABLE VALLEY UPHILL
Answer: The bird never got upset or perturbed and was always composed. He was—UNFLAPPABLE

110. **Jumbles:** LINER HENCE ACQUIT ACIDIC
Answer: The reindeer ate the growth on the tree bark and were—"LICHEN" IT

111. **Jumbles:** COLOR LEVEL SANDAL BIOPSY
Answer: Dracula started paying for plasma because he knew that—BLOOD "SELLS"

112. **Jumbles:** GUEST BRISK FRIGID BROKEN
Answer: The fascinating documentary about frogs was—"RIBBITING"

113. **Jumbles:** HUNCH TRUTH LEGEND IGUANA
Answer: How do they say hello in the Alps?—"HIGH" THERE

114. **Jumbles:** ADAGE ICIER TUNNEL EXPORT
Answer: With so much dental work needed, they joked about having an orthodontist—ON RETAINER

115. **Jumbles:** VALET IGLOO SEESAW PEACHY
Answer: When not one person bid in the charity auction, the host thought—WHAT GIVES?

116. **Jumbles:** SWIFT SHIFT ADVENT BRAZEN
Answer: He lost after going "all in" and had to give his wife the—FIRST-HAND NEWS

117. **Jumbles:** NOVEL GOUGE GROWTH HAIRDO
Answer: She wanted to get a new, more modern scale. They'd had theirs—"WEIGH" TOO LONG

118. **Jumbles:** YOUTH TULIP CHOPPY STRAND
Answer: When the owls made their plans, they were—IN CAHOOTS

119. **Jumbles:** SWUNG MOUTH COSTLY WEAKLY
Answer: They studied the attractive properties of certain metals at the—MAGNET SCHOOL

120. **Jumbles:** YEAST POISE MAGPIE FORBID
Answer: Big Ben rings on a regular basis with the—PASSAGE OF TIME

121. **Jumbles:** LLAMA FOAMY SUDDEN LIKELY
Answer: The garbage dump overflowed when the—LAND FILLED

122. **Jumbles:** SUSHI LEMUR STOOGE FLIGHT
Answer: The conch soup was quite expensive, but customers were happy to—SHELL OUT FOR IT

123. **Jumbles:** HANDY QUIRK FLAVOR LEGEND
Answer: Most people would have helped the stranded motorist, but he wasn't that—KIND OF A GUY

124. **Jumbles:** CABLE SLASH TARIFF WALLOP
Answer: The new restaurant chain offered a healthful menu at all of their—"LOW-CALS"

125. **Jumbles:** VENUE TEPID WEAKLY HANGAR
Answer: When asphalt became commonly used on roads, it—PAVED THE WAY

126. **Jumbles:** LUNCH NEWLY DEFACE IMPAIR
Answer: The nurse was trying to do his job, but the patient was being extremely—ILL-MANNERED

127. **Jumbles:** WEARY DOUBT TYCOON OXYGEN
Answer: The circles built a community with public transportation so they could—GET AROUND TOWN

128. **Jumbles:** PENNY SWISH GARLIC GROOVY
Answer: The new plant nursery was experiencing—GROWING PAINS

129. **Jumbles:** ABACK TEMPT DREAMY SHRINK
Answer: The Lincoln penny debuted on the centennial of his birth because—IT MADE "CENTS"

130. **Jumbles:** ALIBI DITTO FOSSIL PRIMER
Answer: When Magellan rounded South America headed for the Pacific, he was in—DIRE STRAITS

131. **Jumbles:** GOURD CHIVE TWENTY SKETCH
Answer: The glue factory employees planned to start a labor union and—STICK TOGETHER

132. **Jumbles:** VALVE TALLY CALMLY BYPASS
Answer: The blood donors didn't mind waiting, because the facility had a—PLASMA TV

133. **Jumbles:** DIMLY SHOWN SMELLY TATTOO
Answer: The moonshiners were getting their photo taken so they—STOOD STILL

134. **Jumbles:** TASTY PITCH SOCKET GALLON
Answer: America's westward expansion in the 1800s took place—IN STAGES

135. **Jumbles:** LIMBO OFTEN IODINE TROPHY
Answer: While strolling with a friend, Robert Frost recited his new composition. It was—POETRY IN MOTION

136. **Jumbles:** OLDER SHINY MUTTER CABANA
Answer: The TV newscasters reported the news from where they were—STATIONED

137. **Jumbles:** GUPPY GOUGE MISFIT TARGET
Answer: The race car driver had his own line of deodorant called—PIT STOP

138. **Jumbles:** EXUDE TAKEN JIGSAW ISLAND
Answer: Filling in all the information on the Internal Revenue Service forms was—TAXING

139. **Jumbles:** MAUVE ELOPE COGNAC JALOPY
Answer: The FBI agents wanted the money launderer to—COME CLEAN

140. **Jumbles:** BRASH TARDY ENZYME CAMPUS
Answer: The stage actors who liked to go fishing together were—CAST MEMBERS

141. **Jumbles:** YACHT SHEEN MAYHEM PACIFY
Answer: When asked if she was enjoying the sweet potatoes, she said—YES, I "YAM"

142. **Jumbles:** OZONE ALIBI DIVERT HUBCAP
Answer: Howard Hughes built the "Spruce Goose" out of wood and was able to—BOARD THE PLANE

143. **Jumbles:** FOYER ABIDE STIGMA SHIFTY
Answer: Can most people correctly pronounce the name of Iceland's capital?—IT'S HARD TO SAY

144. **Jumbles:** FRAME SHRUG BRUNCH COMPLY
Answer: When both dogs went after the ball at the same time, the ball was—UP FOR GRABS

145. **Jumbles:** GLORY INEPT RELENT BORDER
Answer: The folklore characters wanted to cross the river but didn't want to use the—"TROLL" BRIDGE

146. **Jumbles:** AGAIN WINCH RIDDLE THWART
Answer: Regarding the invention of latex surgical gloves in 1894, William Halstead—HAD A HAND IN IT

147. **Jumbles:** UTTER SENSE TIGHTS RABBIT
Answer: The ram friends, who loved to smash their heads together, were—BEST "BUTTIES"

148. **Jumbles:** ANKLE TIGER NIMBLE PSYCHE
Answer: When scientist Albert Ghiorso added to the periodic table, he was—IN HIS ELEMENT

149. **Jumbles:** SIGHT TIPSY SMOOTH PIRATE
Answer: The construction of the staircase wasn't going well because of all the—MISSTEPS

150. **Jumbles:** SLIMY NUDGE DEPICT SPRAIN
Answer: The rain made it hard for the ghost to haunt people, but it didn't—DAMPEN HIS SPIRIT

151. **Jumbles:** TURBO WAGER PUDDLE ORNERY
Answer: The bottom of the valley was a little further—DOWN THE ROAD

152. **Jumbles:** SLOSH CHIDE PLURAL CACTUS
Answer: She loved having the new way of discarding food scraps in the sink—AT HER DISPOSAL

153. **Jumbles:** AMUSE GRIND THORNY FREEZE
Answer: She tried not eating for a few days to lose weight, but for her, it couldn't—END FAST ENOUGH

154. **Jumbles:** LIMBO OUNCE UNLESS THRASH
Answer: The French cheese makers were always happy to take time to—SHOOT THE "BRIES"

155. **Jumbles:** CABLE VIVID GATHER INHALE
Answer: If George Washington's Mount Rushmore carving came to life, he'd—HAVE A BIG HEAD

156. **Jumbles:** CELLO KNACK CRAFTY MUTTER
Answer: The pair of scissors was defective and didn't—MAKE THE CUT

157. **Jumbles:** MERCY NIPPY JOYOUS MARVEL
Answer: She was learning synonyms for "large," and loved it—IMMENSELY

158. **Jumbles:** GOING BUNCH RETIRE HELIUM
Answer: The food truck parked along the side of the road was able to—CURB HUNGER

159. **Jumbles:** HIPPO HONEY FRIGHT STUCCO
Answer: The difficult decision between going with glossy or matte prints was a—PHOTO FINISH

160. **Jumbles:** GUILD AROSE CASINO SPIRAL
Answer: When she found out how many calories were in her can of cola, it was—"SODA-PRESSING"

161. **Jumbles:** BOTTLE OUTLAW DIVIDE BEADLE MISLAY FECUND
Answer: What a belly dancer can be expected to do—TWIDDLE HER MIDDLE

162. **Jumbles:** BOUNTY HELIUM CRABBY SLOGAN TALKER APATHY
Answer: "May I introduce you to my husband?"—"THAT'S A LOT OF BULL"

163. **Jumbles:** BELONG HAUNCH CANYON WOEFUL NOBODY FORAGE
Answer: Why you should get up before daylight when you're trying to find the answer to a tough problem—IT'LL SOON DAWN ON YOU

164. **Jumbles:** NOVICE AFLOAT TRYING PEWTER MATRON BRANCH
Answer: You should take a number at that popular pastry shop in order to keep this—YOUR "WAIT" UNDER CONTROL

165. **Jumbles:** NESTLE GALLEY FOURTH MYOPIC BUTLER HECTIC
Answer: Could this be another name for all the mail that's on its way to those congressmen?— "CAPITOL" LETTERS

166. **Jumbles:** OVERDO HAMPER CARNAL MEMORY NUMBER PIGEON
Answer: What the boy scout said when he fixed the horn on the little old lady's bicycle—"BEEP REPAIRED"

167. **Jumbles:** GAMBLE INDUCT ALPACA LOTION DEFACE NICELY
Answer: Nothing gets a person all up in the air quicker than this—AN INFLATED EGO

168. **Jumbles:** GLOOMY CLOVER VERMIN OBLIGE AERATE LAWYER
Answer: That ancient statue phoned his insurance broker because he need this—MORE "COVERAGE"

169. **Jumbles:** GROTTO EMBARK PARITY MAROON LACKEY RELISH
Answer: What the stingy rich uncle was—A "CLOSE" RELATION

170. **Jumbles:** DEBATE EXEMPT ALKALI LUNACY SUBWAY RAGLAN
Answer: That practical joker shakes your hand one minute and—PULLS YOUR LEG THE NEXT

171. **Jumbles:** MAINLY COMEDY BUTTER DONKEY PACKET THEORY
Answer: How the other animals expressed their respect for the giraffe—THEY LOOKED UP TO HIM

172. **Jumbles:** DAINTY SHAKEN PEWTER COWARD TROPHY MALADY
Answer: Although he knew his job "backwards and forwards," he was fired—AND THAT WAS WHY

173. **Jumbles:** BEETLE MORTAR INSIST DETAIN TACKLE PULPIT
Answer: "Have you found out the source of that moonshine yet?"—"IT'S A SECRET STILL"

174. **Jumbles:** LIQUID INFECT BUBBLE ARTERY CROTCH MODEST
Answer: When he saw the woman of his dreams, he was this—FIT TO BE "TIED"

175. **Jumbles:** INHALE STRONG INVOKE MARVEL GROGGY INFAMY
Answer: When they collected Easter eggs together, it was a—FAMILY GATHERING

176. **Jumbles:** SHROUD GRUMPY POETIC FILLET SALARY CANNED
Answer: The chef was at the point in the food preparation where it was—"THYME" FOR SEASONING

177. **Jumbles:** FATHOM ABRUPT OUTLAW DEFINE SHAKEN HUMBLE
Answer: You can see Abraham Lincoln on Mount Rushmore if you—HEAD FOR THE HILLS

178. **Jumbles:** STRING MAYHEM ODDEST REVOLT HEALTH FLEECE
Answer: When her children all chipped in to buy her a gold necklace, she—HIT THE MOTHER LODE

179. **Jumbles:** HEAVEN QUIRKY CONFER BITTER MODULE TROWEL
Answer: Exploring Alaska for its natural resources in the 1800s was difficult, but that—CAME WITH THE TERRITORY

180. **Jumbles:** VERBAL BOUNCY DISMAY FORGOT FELINE SPRAWL
Answer: The car dealership put up new billboards to—DRIVE MORE TRAFFIC

Need More Jumbles®?

Order any of these books through your bookseller or call Triumph Books toll-free at 800-888-4741.

Jumble® Books

More than 175 puzzles each!

Cowboy Jumble®
$10.95 • ISBN: 978-1-62937-355-3

Jammin' Jumble®
$9.95 • ISBN: 978-1-57243-844-6

Java Jumble®
$10.95 • ISBN: 978-1-60078-415-6

Jet Set Jumble®
$9.95 • ISBN: 978-1-60078-353-1

Jolly Jumble®
$10.95 • ISBN: 978-1-60078-214-5

Jumble® Anniversary
$10.95 • ISBN: 987-1-62937-734-6

Jumble® Ballet
$10.95 • ISBN: 978-1-62937-616-5

Jumble® Birthday
$10.95 • ISBN: 978-1-62937-652-3

Jumble® Celebration
$10.95 • ISBN: 978-1-60078-134-6

Jumble® Champion
$10.95 • ISBN: 978-1-62937-870-1

Jumble® Christmas
$10.95 • ISBN: 978-1-63727-182-7

Jumble® Coronation
$10.95 • ISBN: 978-1-62937-976-0

Jumble® Cuisine
$10.95 • ISBN: 978-1-62937-735-3

Jumble® Drag Race
$9.95 • ISBN: 978-1-62937-483-3

Jumble® Ever After
$10.95 • ISBN: 978-1-62937-785-8

Jumble® Explorer
$9.95 • ISBN: 978-1-60078-854-3

Jumble® Explosion
$10.95 • ISBN: 978-1-60078-078-3

Jumble® Fever
$9.95 • ISBN: 978-1-57243-593-3

Jumble® Galaxy
$10.95 • ISBN: 978-1-60078-583-2

Jumble® Garden
$10.95 • ISBN: 978-1-62937-653-0

Jumble® Genius
$10.95 • ISBN: 978-1-57243-896-5

Jumble® Geography
$10.95 • ISBN: 978-1-62937-615-8

Jumble® Getaway
$10.95 • ISBN: 978-1-60078-547-4

Jumble® Gold
$10.95 • ISBN: 978-1-62937-354-6

Jumble® Health
$10.95 • ISBN: 978-1-63727-085-1

Jumble® Jackpot
$10.95 • ISBN: 978-1-57243-897-2

Jumble® Jailbreak
$9.95 • ISBN: 978-1-62937-002-6

Jumble® Jambalaya
$9.95 • ISBN: 978-1-60078-294-7

Jumble® Jitterbug
$10.95 • ISBN: 978-1-60078-584-9

Jumble® Journey
$10.95 • ISBN: 978-1-62937-549-6

Jumble® Jubilation
$10.95 • ISBN: 978-1-62937-784-1

Jumble® Jubilee
$10.95 • ISBN: 978-1-57243-231-4

Jumble® Juggernaut
$9.95 • ISBN: 978-1-60078-026-4

Jumble® Kingdom
$10.95 • ISBN: 978-1-62937-079-8

Jumble® Knockout
$9.95 • ISBN: 978-1-62937-078-1

Jumble® Madness
$10.95 • ISBN: 978-1-892049-24-7

Jumble® Magic
$9.95 • ISBN: 978-1-60078-795-9

Jumble® Mania
$10.95 • ISBN: 978-1-57243-697-8

Jumble® Marathon
$9.95 • ISBN: 978-1-60078-944-1

Jumble® Masterpiece
$10.95 • ISBN: 978-1-62937-916-6

Jumble® Neighbor
$10.95 • ISBN: 978-1-62937-845-9

Jumble® Parachute
$10.95 • ISBN: 978-1-62937-548-9

Jumble® Party
$10.95 • ISBN: 978-1-63727-008-0

Jumble® Safari
$9.95 • ISBN: 978-1-60078-675-4

Jumble® Sensation
$10.95 • ISBN: 978-1-60078-548-1

Jumble® Skyscraper
$10.95 • ISBN: 978-1-62937-869-5

Jumble® Symphony
$10.95 • ISBN: 978-1-62937-131-3

Jumble® Theater
$9.95 • ISBN: 978-1-62937-484-0

Jumble® Time Machine: 1972
$10.95 • ISBN: 978-1-63727-082-0

Jumble® Trouble
$10.95 • ISBN: 978-1-62937-917-3

Jumble® University
$10.95 • ISBN: 978-1-62937-001-9

Jumble® Unleashed
$10.95 • ISBN: 978-1-62937-844-2

Jumble® Vacation
$10.95 • ISBN: 978-1-60078-796-6

Jumble® Wedding
$9.95 • ISBN: 978-1-62937-307-2

Jumble® Workout
$10.95 • ISBN: 978-1-60078-943-4

Jump, Jive and Jumble®
$9.95 • ISBN: 978-1-60078-215-2

Lunar Jumble®
$9.95 • ISBN: 978-1-60078-853-6

Monster Jumble®
$10.95 • ISBN: 978-1-62937-213-6

Mystic Jumble®
$9.95 • ISBN: 978-1-62937-130-6

Rainy Day Jumble®
$10.95 • ISBN: 978-1-60078-352-4

Royal Jumble®
$10.95 • ISBN: 978-1-60078-738-6

Sports Jumble®
$10.95 • ISBN: 978-1-57243-113-3

Summer Fun Jumble®
$10.95 • ISBN: 978-1-57243-114-0

Touchdown Jumble®
$9.95 • ISBN: 978-1-62937-212-9

Oversize Jumble® Books

More than 500 puzzles!

Colossal Jumble®
$19.95 • ISBN: 978-1-57243-490-5

Jumbo Jumble®
$19.95 • ISBN: 978-1-57243-314-4

Jumble® Crosswords™

More than 175 puzzles!

Jumble® Crosswords™
$10.95 • ISBN: 978-1-57243-347-2